MW01489949

Discover the Magic:

The Ultimate Insider's Guide to Walt Disney World

By: Roger Wilk

Copyright Notice

© **2015 Roger Wilk**

All rights reserved. This material may not be reproduced, displayed, modified or distributed without the express prior written permission of the copyright holder.

This book is not affiliated in any way with Walt Disney World or the Disney Company.

Also by Roger Wilk...

Disney Tips & Secrets: Unlocking the Magic of a Walt Disney World Vacation

Experience a magical Disney vacation- updated and EXPANDED with 240 tips and secrets to save time and MONEY while taking the stress out of your Disney vacation. Whether you're going to The Magic Kingdom, Animal Kingdom, Hollywood Studios, or Epcot, we've got you covered! Discover hidden paths and a secret exit from The Magic Kingdom. Beat the crowds as you head for the monorail back to the parking lots or your hotel. Learn the secrets to vacation photos and **so much more!**
Get Disney Tips & Secrets today!!!

Disney Christmas Magic: The Ultimate Insider's Guide to Spending the Holidays at Walt Disney World

Experience the happiest place on Earth during the most magical season on Earth- the Christmas holiday season! Learn all about the special holiday events at Walt Disney World like Mickey's Very Merry Christmas Party at Magic Kingdom, Epcot's Candlelight Processional, and the Osborne Family Spectacle of Dancing Lights at Hollywood Studios. All this and more awaits!
Discover Disney Christmas Magic today!!!

Keys to the Kingdom: Your Complete Guide to Walt Disney World's Magic Kingdom Theme Park

Prepare to experience the crown jewel of Disney parks. Prepare to be enchanted by the **Magic Kingdom!**
In **Keys to the Kingdom** you'll find everything you need to make the most of your Disney vacation including detailed maps, ride guides, dining guides, and **more**! You'll also get complete guides to Magic Kingdom's awesome shows & parades. Neatly organized and supported by nearly 70 photos, maps, and charts, the **Keys to the Kingdom** are ready to unlock the magic of **your** Disney vacation!

To your family

With the hope that this book will help you create as many magical memories as I've had the privilege of sharing with my family.

Table of Contents

1) INTRODUCTION 9

   ABOUT THIS EDITION 10

2) DISNEY VACATION PLANNING 15

   WHEN TO VISIT...15

      Really Busy...16

      Busy 16

      Moderate to light...16

   FLORIDA WEATHER 18

   OTHER FACTORS..19

   THE ABSOLUTE BEST (AND WORST) TIMES TO GO 20

   HOW LONG TO STAY...24

   ON DISNEY PROPERTY OR OFF? 26

      Advantages of staying on Disney property 28

      Disadvantages of staying on Disney property 29

      Advantages of staying off Disney property................31

      Disadvantages of staying off Disney property 31

3) DISNEY TICKET INFORMATION......................................33

   DISNEY TICKET PRICES AND OPTIONS 35

      Magic Your Way 36

      Park Hopper...37

      Water Park Fun & More...38

      Why not both?..39

      Let's do the math...40

   UNDERSTANDING DISNEY'S FASTPASS+ SYSTEM...................41

      FastPass+ tips 45

4) ORLANDO RESORTS, HOTELS, & OTHER ACCOMMODATIONS 47

   DISNEY WORLD RESORT CATEGORIES 47

      Disney Deluxe Resorts...48

      Disney Moderate Resorts.......................................49

      Disney Value Reports 50

      Disney Deluxe Villas 50

   DISNEY DELUXE RESORTS TOP PICKS 51

      Disney's Yacht Club Resort and Beach Club Resort.....51

Disney's Animal Kingdom Lodge..*53*
Disney Boardwalk Inn *54*
Disney's Polynesian Village Resort...*58*
Other Disney Deluxe Resorts *61*
DISNEY MODERATE RESORTS..*62*
Disney's Port Orleans Resort – French Quarter...........................*62*
Disney's Caribbean Beach Resort...*64*
Other moderate Disney resorts...*65*
DISNEY VALUE RESORTS *65*
Disney's Pop Century Resort *66*
Disney's All Star Sports Resort *68*
Disney's Art of Animation Resort *70*
Other Disney Value Resorts *72*
DISNEY DELUXE VILLAS *72*
Disney's Old Key West Resort *73*
The Villas at Disney's Wilderness Lodge *75*
Other Disney Deluxe Villa Resorts..*76*
STAYING OFF DISNEY PROPERTY...*77*
Which location is best?..*78*
Other things to consider when staying offsite *79*
Orlando area 'best bets' *80*

5) WALT DISNEY WORLD THEME PARKS **89**

MAGIC KINGDOM...*90*
Main Street, U.S.A...*91*
Adventureland *93*
Frontierland *94*
Liberty Square...*94*
Fantasyland *95*
Tomorrowland *96*
Magic Kingdom "Can't Miss" rides and attractions....................*97*
EPCOT...*109*
Future World Pavilions...*111*
Epcot World Showcase *116*
Epcot "Can't Miss" rides and attractions.................................*121*
HOLLYWOOD STUDIOS *128*
Hollywood Boulevard..*131*
Echo Lake *132*
Streets of America *133*
Mickey Avenue...*134*

Animation Courtyard 135
Pixar Place 135
Sunset Boulevard 136
Hollywood Studios "Can't Miss" rides and attractions 137
ANIMAL KINGDOM 144
Lands of Animal Kingdom 145
Animal Kingdom "Can't Miss" rides and attractions 149

6) WALT DISNEY WORLD WATER PARKS 155

TYPHOON LAGOON 156
Top Attractions at Typhoon Lagoon 158
BLIZZARD BEACH 162
Top Attractions at Blizzard Beach............................165

7) READY, SET, GO! 171

Note from the author:

First and foremost, I'd like to say "Thank You!" for purchasing this paperback version of Discover the Magic. Independent authors like me could not make it without the support of readers like you, and for that I am eternally grateful.

Based on feedback I've seen from other reviewers, you may be surprised (and disappointed) to discover that the images in the paperback version of this book are in black and white. Believe me- I am too! Although I take quite a bit of time to ensure the preview version of the paperback displays in black and white on Amazon, it seems many readers view the Kindle preview with color images. Although I have also added a note in the book description indicating the paperback images are in black and white, many readers do not realize that until their book is delivered, and are ultimately disappointed. After all, Walt Disney World is full of bright and beautiful colors, and you want to experience the images in all their full-color glory!

Unfortunately, the prohibitively high cost of color printing just does not make that possible. For example, a book this size would cost me about $25 per copy to produce in color, and at that price (just to break even) I don't think I'd sell many copies. In hope of reaching as many readers as possible, I try to price my books as low as I possibly can, and to do that, I can only publish the paperback versions in black and white.

There are a couple of ways that you can see the images of this book the way they are meant to be seen- in full color. One way is to utilize Amazon's Kindle MatchBook program. This allows anyone who purchases the paperback version of the book to purchase the Kindle version for only $.99. You only need the free Kindle app, available for iPhone, Android, and Windows platforms.

I will also be soon publishing full-color high resolution images of all the photos in this book on my blog at www.DisneyVacations4Families.com. Check there, or on my Twitter page (@Disney4Families) to find out when the online versions are available.

Thanks again for reading, and for your support. Have a magical day!

1) Introduction

Enjoy a magical vacation to Walt Disney World

Congratulations! You're going to Disney World! Or at least you're thinking about it- otherwise you wouldn't be reading this book. Whether you've already booked your trip, or even if you're just considering a visit to Walt Disney World in Orlando, you've come to the right place. If you've already booked your trip, this Disney vacation guide will provide everything you need to know to make the most of your Disney vacation. If you're still just 'thinking' about going, the details on these pages will help you make an educated decision as to whether Disney World is really the place for you. Call it a hunch, but I think you'll decide to do it!

I'll provide tips on how to plan your Disney vacation- whether you're flying or driving, and whether you're staying on or off of Disney property. I'll help you decide which ticket options are right for you by providing details on the many Disney ticket options available. Believe me, it's not quite as simple as just going online or calling to purchase your tickets. There are several options available, and considering the substantial amount of money that you'll be plunking down for the purchase, you'll want to make sure you get the right tickets for you and your family or traveling companions.

I'll provide expanded overviews of all the Disney parks and attractions, and provide tips to help you decide where to go, when to go, and how long to stay. Since the magic of Walt Disney World doesn't start or end at the Magic Kingdom, I'll provide the details you need to enjoy ALL of Disney's great parks and attractions. If you only have time to visit some (or all) of Disney's major theme parks, this book will provide the details you need to make the most of your visit. If you have time to visit their awesome water parks (which I'd HIGHLY recommend) I'll provide all the information you need to make the most of those visits too!

About this edition

Back in 2012 when I published the first edition of Discover the Magic, (and my first book ever) I had no idea how much enjoyment and success I'd have as an author. I remember discussing the idea to write a book with my wife. She was hesitant and said, "Who is going to read it?" My thought process was similar to a line from the Field of Dreams movie: "If you write it, they will read." I was optimistic that somebody would be interested in what I had to say and hopeful that my passion for, and knowledge of Walt Disney World would be useful to readers considering a Disney vacation.

Now, going on three years, three additional titles, tens of thousands of copies later, here I am. Back where it all started with the 2nd edition of "Discover the Magic". I'm thrilled with the fact that thousands of readers like you, with a desire to learn more about the magical experience of a vacation to Walt Disney World, will take the time and spend their hard-earned dollars to buy or borrow this book. I'll do my best to give you your money's worth!

Prepare for your magical adventure

In this expanded and updated version of Discover the Magic, all new for 2015, you'll get even more magic than ever before. In fact, updates that started off as a minor refresh have evolved into a major rewrite. I had originally intended this 2nd edition to be an update of everything that has changed at Disney since the first edition was released in May of 2012. That in itself would have been an extensive facelift. However, as I began writing, I realized there was so much more to say and so much more to cover than I did with the original. The original version was about 15,000 words and this edition is about double that- right around 30,000 words. While this has delayed publication by several weeks, you the reader will reap the benefits!

I'm adding expanded coverage of all the parks and attractions, and updating the original edition with all the latest developments and changes at Walt Disney World. Disney World is always changing and expanding, and this book will fill you in on what's new- and what's coming! You'll find details on the newest attractions like those in the New Fantasyland at Magic Kingdom, and I'll update you on the expansions planned at Hollywood Studios and Animal Kingdom too.

I'll also provide everything you'll need to know to make the most of Disney's most recent customer service innovation- the new FastPass+ reservation system. In the hotels section, you'll find expanded coverage of the various Disney resorts, and a look at additional offsite hotels, condos, and other resorts to enjoy if you choose to stay off property. Unlike some of the other Disney travel authors out there, I'm not going to tell you that you MUST stay at a Disney resort on Disney property. I'll provide an overview of the options and discuss the pros and cons of each so YOU can make the decision that's right for YOU!

In addition to the many changes I've mentioned above, I've also refreshed many of the photos in the original book, and added tons of new ones too. In fact, this edition now has over 150 full-color photos, graphs and charts. Compare this to what you'll find in many other Disney travel guides, many of which have no images at all, and I think you'll agree the pictures really do help tell the story. After all, what good would a Disney travel guide be without lots of pretty pictures?

The happiest place on Earth

If you enjoy this book, please check out my other books: Disney Tips & Secrets, Disney Christmas Magic, and Keys to the Kingdom- my complete guide to Disney's Magic Kingdom theme park, available in both the Kindle format and in paperback.

Prepare yourself for the journey of a lifetime. No matter where you go in the world, you'll never find a place that quite captures the magic of Walt Disney World. From the time you arrive at the Transportation and Ticketing Center

(TTC) at Magic Kingdom until the time you return to your car or to the airport after you leave the last park at the end of your trip, you'll feel as if you are truly on a magical adventure. Throughout your trip you'll be creating memories that last a lifetime.

Enough talk, it's time to begin our journey. So relax, enjoy, and **Let the Memories Begin!!!**

2) Disney Vacation Planning

If you're thinking about a Walt Disney World vacation, one of the keys to a successful trip is in the planning. A Disney trip is not the type of vacation where you can just get up and go. If you want to make the most of your trip to the Orlando area, you'll want to plan ahead. Planning a Disney vacation does **not** need to be stressful either! Sometimes, planning is half the fun. By reading this book you're already off to a great start!

When to Visit

Your schedule may dictate the time of year you're able to visit Walt Disney World. School schedules, work schedules, and family events all play a part in determining when you can visit Magic Kingdom and the other theme parks at Walt Disney World. If you have flexibility in your schedule, here's a look at the crowds you can expect at various times throughout the year.

Christmas is one of the busiest times to visit Disney

Really Busy

- The week before Christmas through New Year's Day
- Easter week and surrounding 'Spring Break' weeks
- Fourth of July week

Busy

- Spring and Summer (other than the weeks mentioned above)
- Thanksgiving week

Moderate to light

- Late February
- Early May

- Mid to late September
- October through early December (except Thanksgiving week)

Expect big crowds at Christmas

There really is no secret to this information. You'll find similar information published in many books, on many blogs, and on countless websites as you begin the journey of preparing for your Disney vacation. Some reviewers have argued that this information is 'common sense' and shouldn't be in this book at all.

I'm writing this book under the assumption that you're beginning your Disney vacation planning from ground zero without having done any other research. If you already know this information- please don't hold it against me. Keep reading, and I promise you you'll find plenty of stuff that you didn't know!

Florida weather

When Walt Disney began scouting new locations for his follow up project to Disneyland in California, one of his requirements was that it be located in an area of the country where it could be open year-round. Given the mild winters in central Florida, he certainly got that! If you're from the U.S., or possibly anywhere on Earth, you may already know that central Florida is hot in the summer. I mean really H-O-T hot! If you're coming from a cooler climate this will be quite an adjustment for you if you're visiting Disney in the heat of the summer. Consider this if you decide to take your trip during the kids' summer vacation.

It's not just hot either- it's very, very, humid. I'm talking drenched with sweat when you walk outside at 8:00 a.m. humid. If you're from Texas, Arizona, or other areas of the southwest, you'll be used to the heat, but chances are you will NOT be accustomed to the humidity of a Florida summer. (Especially later in the summer in the July-August timeframe.)

Another factor to consider if you plan a Disney vacation in the summer is the rain. The heat and humidity of the Florida summer bring rain and thunderstorms nearly every day. The good news is that in most cases it's not the 'rain all day and ruin your vacation' rain, it's more like periods of 'brief showers that cool the temps 10 degrees and feel really, really good when you're hot' rain. Never fear, the clouds will clear and the temps (and humidity) will go right back to where they were before the storms.

According to Weather.com, here's a look at the average temperatures and rainfall you can expect during your Disney vacation:

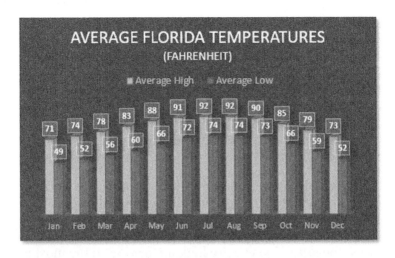

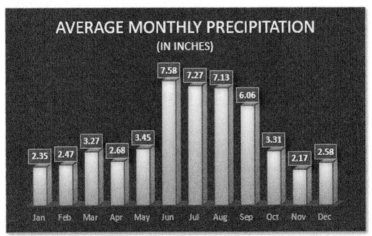

Other factors

Coincidentally, the busy seasons are also the time when accommodations & transportation are most expensive. If you go during one of the less-crowded times you're sure to save some money and get more from your park visits with the help of shorter lines.

Keep in mind that some of the attractions may be closed for repairs during winter months & off-seasons, and also some of the park hours may be shortened. For example Disney's fantastic water parks, Typhoon Lagoon and Blizzard Beach usually have their maintenance done during these times. At times both parks will be open, but several of the slides may be closed for maintenance. Also, during December and January one of the water parks may be closed completely.

Check the Disney website for park hours, closures, and scheduled maintenance closings for some of the key attractions. You'd hate to spend all this time and money planning and making your trip reservations only to find out one of the attractions you're looking forward to the most is closed. To Disney's credit, these closures are scheduled well in advance allowing you plenty of time to plan around them.

The absolute BEST (and worst) times to go

Throughout this book, I'll provide many details about Disney vacations and Walt Disney World that are purely based on facts. I can tell you about the parks. I can tell you about the attractions. I can list the shows and ticket prices. Much of that information you can find in various bits and pieces elsewhere if you do enough digging, and some of it you'll find anywhere and everywhere.

However, much of this book, and all of my books really, is my personal take on things. My advice and opinions based on my own personal experiences. My own tips based on what I've learned throughout my many, many trips to Disney over the years. At times I will provide information that is 100% completely my opinion based on my personal experiences and nothing else. This is one of those times.

The absolute BEST time to visit Walt Disney World is the Christmas season! The absolute WORST time? The Christmas season! Huh? Say what? Please bear with me and let me explain...

There's nothing quite like Cinderella Castle at Christmas

There is no time at Disney that is more magical than the Christmas season. This is what makes it the best time of year to visit Disney. The lights, the decorations, and the special events such as Mickey's Very Merry Christmas Party at Magic Kingdom, and the Candlelight Processional at Epcot, make it more memorable and exciting than any other time of year. When you stroll through the gates at Magic Kingdom and are greeted by thousands of poinsettias, wreaths, and other holiday decorations, you'll realize that things are quite a bit different than any other time of year. When you're smack dab in the center of Main Street U.S.A. during the Castle lighting ceremony, you'll realize that a Disney Christmas is unlike any other. When you visit Hollywood Studios and see MILLIONS of Christmas lights dancing to the beat of the music at the

Osborne Family Spectacle of Dancing Lights, you'll know
that Disney at Christmas is the place to be!

Seeing is believing at the Osborne Family Spectacle of Dancing Lights

Of course now that you (and millions of others) know this,
you'll understand why the Christmas season can be the
absolute WORST time of the year to visit Walt Disney
World- the crowds! If you visit Disney after the kids get out
for Christmas break, or even worse during the week
between Christmas and New Year's, you can expect wall-to-
wall packed to the brim crowds just about everywhere you
go. Some days the Magic Kingdom is so crowded that
Disney actually has to close the park to new guests because
they reach capacity!

While some may find the crowds actually add to the festive
atmosphere of Christmas, others- especially those that get
uneasy or claustrophobic in large crowds, may find this to
be a terrible experience. Know that if you go during this
time you'll have longer lines for everything you do. You'll
have to arrive early to get a good viewing spot for the
parades and fireworks, and you'll pay peak prices for
everything from airfare to hotels to rental cars.

If you've never visited Walt Disney World, I wouldn't advise going during the week between Christmas and New Year's for your first Disney experience. It will simply be too overwhelming and due to the large crowds, you'll end up missing out on a lot of things that you'd enjoy much more at other, less crowded times of year. If you've been to Disney a few times, have ridden the rides and seen the shows and attractions at least once, but want to experience Christmas 'Disney style', then by all means consider it if it fits into your plans. It will definitely be an experience you'll never forget!

So what do you do if you truly want to experience a Disney Christmas, but absolutely do NOT want the hustle and bustle of the huge crowds? There's still a way to do this... Shhhhh. Don't tell...

Disney begins transforming Walt Disney World from Halloween to Christmas on November 1st. In fact if you travel during this time of year, you'll have the opportunity to go to Mickey's Not So Scary Halloween Party in late October, plus get a taste of the Christmas season in early November as the transformation begins. The holiday transformation of Magic Kingdom will be complete by the opening night of Mickey's Very Merry Christmas Party, usually the first weekend in November, and the rest of the decorations will be completed at the other parks and resorts of Walt Disney World by the day after Thanksgiving.

If you want the complete Disney experience, without the crazy crowds, head to Orlando any time between the Monday AFTER Thanksgiving thru the 2nd week of December (when the kids usually get out for Christmas break). The crowds will be much more manageable, the weather will be slightly warmer, and you'll still get to experience everything that makes Disney the most magical place on earth! In addition, airfare, hotels, and rental cars will be much cheaper than they will between mid-December and New Year's Day.

Don't miss the Candlelight Processional at Epcot

Depending on how the calendar falls, you may have the opportunity to enjoy Disney Christmas magic AFTER New Year's Day too! The Christmas decorations will be up until the weekend after New Year's, and the crowds will be much smaller after January 1st. Some of the special Christmas events such as Mickey's Christmas party at Magic Kingdom and Epcot's Holidays Around the World and Candlelight Processional will have concluded by then, but you'll still have the opportunity to enjoy the glorious Osborne Family Spectacle of Dancing Lights at Hollywood Studios and all the Christmas decorations throughout the parks and resorts.

How long to stay

If you're taking your first trip to Walt Disney World and plan to visit all four theme parks, you'll probably want to plan at least a seven day vacation. This will give you at least one full day at each park, and allow you to visit a couple of your favorites more than once. On our typical Disney visit of 7-10 days, we usually visit Magic Kingdom at least three times!

The Water Park Fun & More option includes DisneyQuest

What's that? You didn't know that Disney World has **four** major theme parks? Don't worry, you're not alone. Many people think that Magic Kingdom IS Walt Disney World and don't realize there are three other theme parks that are part of Disney World too! The four theme parks that make up Walt Disney World are: Magic Kingdom (the original park... the one with the big castle) which opened in 1971, Epcot, which opened in 1982, Disney's Hollywood Studios (1989), and Animal Kingdom which opened in 1998.

Another factor to consider when deciding on the length of your stay, is whether or not you are planning to visit Disney's awesome water parks. (Which I'd highly recommend!) Disney's Typhoon Lagoon and Blizzard

Beach are a great way too cool off after spending part of the day in the hot Florida sun. You can get a great deal on tickets to these parks if you select the Water Park Fun & More option when purchasing your Disney tickets. (I'll explain that a bit more in the Disney Ticket Information section.)

No matter how long you're planning to stay in the Orlando area, you'll want to build some 'down time' into your vacation schedule. You can easily walk five miles a day in any of the parks, and a day spent in the hot Florida sun can be simply exhausting. If for example you decide on a 7-day vacation, you'd probably want to purchase a 4 or 5 day park pass- depending on your arrival and departure schedule. This way you can build a 'day off' into your trip to recover from your adventures. Having that break in the middle of your week is sure to make the rest of your stay that much more enjoyable!

On Disney property or off?

Walt Disney World and the Orlando area have a great variety in types and prices of accommodations with an option to fit every budget. Whether you're searching for a luxury hotel with all the amenities, or a budget campground, you're sure to find an option that's just right for you. Before deciding exactly where you'll stay, you need to decide if you want to stay on Disney property, or off-site at one of the many hotels, condos, rental homes, or campgrounds in the Orlando area.

Considering the fact that Walt Disney World is a vacation destination that prides itself on being a family destination, when we first started traveling to Disney we were a bit miffed to discover the limited options available for families with more than two children. Disney has made great strides in this area in recent years, but larger families are still a bit limited in where they can stay.

If you have three kids, or if you're planning on bringing along a friend, you'll find that a third of Disney hotels do not allow more than four to a room. Also, many of the one-bedroom villa options available at Disney resorts (such as Boardwalk Villas and Beach Club Villas) only allow four to a room. Although two bedroom villas (that sleep up to eight) are available at these resorts, they run about $400 more per night than the one-bedroom option. This will price them beyond the reach of many families of five. If you're traveling with five or more, this will definitely be a factor that may steer you toward one of the off-property options in the area.

Disney's Contemporary Resort offers Monorail transportation

Here's a look at some advantages and disadvantages of both options.

Advantages of staying on Disney property

- No rental car needed – Disney provides free transportation to and from the airport, theme parks, water parks, and Downtown Disney.
- If you do rent a car, or drive your own vehicle to Disney, you'll get free parking at the Disney parks. This works out great for us, because often we'd rather drive to the parks then wait for the Disney bus. The free parking perk of staying on property saves us nearly $20 per day in parking fees.
- Bypass baggage claim – The Disney Magical Express will transport your luggage from the airport directly to your hotel room.
- Extra Magic Hours – Walt Disney World visitors staying on Disney property have the benefit of extended theme park hours called Extra Magic Hours on select days at each of the four major theme parks: Magic Kingdom, Animal Kingdom, Epcot, and Hollywood Studios.
- Disney dining plan – The dining plan allows you to pre-purchase your meals at Disney hotels and theme parks which can save you money in the long run.
- Earlier reservations – If you're staying on-property you can book your FastPass+ and dining reservations further in advance than if you're staying off property. In fact with some Disney restaurants such as Be Our Guest at Magic Kingdom, the only way you even have a prayer of landing a dinner reservation is to stay on-property and by booking your trip 6 months in advance.
- Package shipping – When you stay at a Disney resort you can have all the souvenirs you purchase in the parks shipped back to your hotel room. This provides a tremendous benefit over carrying your packages around the theme parks all day.
- More immersive experience – Each and every one of the Disney resorts are decorated in a unique theme that

becomes an integral part of the overall Disney experience.

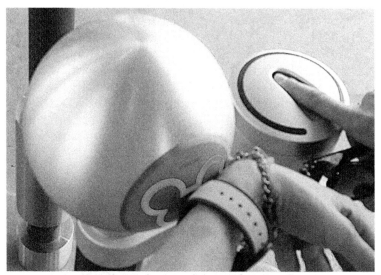

Magic Bands are stylish AND functional!

- You get these super-cool Magic Bands to wear around your resort and the parks during your stay. Not only are they stylish, but they're functional too. They are your all-access ticket at each park entrance, throughout the parks and FastPass+ lines, and for shopping too! Just tap the magic Mickey at any restaurant, gift shop, or Disney store, enter your PIN, and you'll be on your way!

Disadvantages of staying on Disney property

- Options are limited for groups of five or more. Although Disney has added a variety of options for families of five in recent years, your choice of accommodations will still be limited. About a third of Disney resorts cannot accommodate groups larger than four- unless you're willing to split into two rooms.

- Disney resorts tend to be much more expensive than similar off-property accommodations.
- Depending on the resort, you may end up walking a long way to the bus stop, or have a long commute to the theme parks of Walt Disney World. Some of the resorts are very large, so even if your room is near a bus stop, you may be on the bus 15 minutes or so before you even leave the resort. Also some resorts, especially the value resorts, are further away from the parks and Downtown Disney so you may be spending quite a bit of time on Disney busses as you traverse from park to park or to and from your hotel.

Staying at a Disney resort may mean spending A LOT of time on busses

- Without a rental car, you'll have limited mobility. If you want to visit any other Orlando area attractions such as Sea World or Universal Orlando, you'll need to take a cab.
- If you have an early flight home, you'll be getting up before dawn. Disney requires you leave for the airport three hours prior to your departure time if you're using their Magical Express transportation.

- The rooms at Walt Disney World resorts are very small compared to similarly priced off-property hotels and resorts in the area.

Advantages of staying off Disney property

- Because you'll probably have your own car, you're free to come and go as you please.
- Some area resorts offer free transportation to and from Disney theme parks and other Orlando area attractions such as Sea World and Universal Studios. Although their service may be limited to specific parks at specific times throughout the day, it will give you a bit of the best of both worlds.
- Rooms sizes for similarly priced hotels can be 1/3 larger (or more) than Disney's rooms.
- There are many rental homes and resort condominiums in the area that provide 1,000+ square feet of living space and sleeping accommodation for six (or more) for the same price as a room at a Disney value resort where you'll get accommodations for four and approximately 450 square feet of space.
- Rental homes and condos offer full kitchens and all of the conveniences of home. You'll spend much less on food from the grocery store that you can cook 'at home' rather than having all of your meals at Disney parks and restaurants.

Disadvantages of staying off Disney property

- Unless you drive to Disney, you're pretty much forced to rent a car. That, and the cost of parking at the theme parks can offset some of the savings of staying offsite.
- After a long day at the parks you may just want to hop on a bus or monorail and be dropped off at your hotel without having to pile into the car and navigate back in the dark.

Off-property options can provide an excellent value

- Even the closest of the off-property resorts are further away from the parks than the farthest onsite Disney resorts.
- Depending on where you stay (the farther away from the parks you are, the cheaper the rooms will be), some of the parks may be a ½ hour drive or more.
- If you buy souvenirs in the parks, you'll be stuck carrying them around with you all day, or you'll have to wait in line at the park's package pickup to pick them up at the end of a long day. It's usually a pretty quick process, but believe me you'll spend enough time waiting in lines without adding one more. (Of course, if you purchase your souvenirs on the way out of the park at the end of the day, you'll avoid this problem.)

I'll talk more about places to stay in the Orlando area in the Disney Hotels & Accommodations section.

3) Disney Ticket Information

After you've booked your flight to Orlando and your Orlando area accommodations, the next step is purchasing your theme park tickets. Sure you could wait and purchase them when you get to Walt Disney World, but aren't you going to be standing in enough lines already without adding one more? You may even be able to get a discount as part of a Disney World vacation package.

Walt Disney World: Where Dreams Come True

Here are some tips for purchasing your Disney park tickets.

- The simplest, safest, and unfortunately most expensive way to purchase your Walt Disney World tickets is through the Disney website, or by phone directly from Disney. You'll pay full price, but at least you'll have peace of mind knowing your tickets will arrive on time with no surprises. If you're staying on-property, you'll also have the option of purchasing your tickets when making your hotel accommodations.
- Another option if you're purchasing through an online travel site such as Expedia, Travelocity, etc. is to purchase your Walt Disney World tickets when you book your trip. A recent price comparison showed a $50 savings per ticket for 7-day passes.
- An Internet search for "Disney tickets" will yield tons of sites selling Disney World Orlando theme park tickets.

Be cautious when using this approach, and be sure to purchase from a reputable dealer. The Internet is full of horror stories of people who purchase multi-day passes only to realize some of the days were used up or they had purchased non-transferable tickets. Use your head! Chances are if the price sounds too good to be true, it probably is!

- That being said, you can find a slight savings at some Disney websites not owned and operated by Walt Disney World. There are plenty of legitimate options for purchasing Disney tickets. Just do your homework and understand that you're accepting a certain amount of risk.

- When comparing ticket prices, be sure you're doing an 'apples to apples' comparison. Some sites include sales tax in their published price, others do not. Some sites add a delivery or processing fee that isn't mentioned until the final step of the check-out process. **Be sure to read the fine print!**

- I'd recommend purchasing from a site that will mail your tickets to your home, and one that offers expedited shipping via FedEx, etc. Some ticket sellers require that you drive to their office in the Orlando area to pick up your tickets. This only complicates matters.

- Be sure to order your tickets far enough in advance so you know you're not waiting until the last minute for your tickets to arrive. You'd hate to have your tickets arrive in the mail at home a day **after** you've arrived at Disney World.

- Check to see if your employer has a relationship with Disney- you may be able to purchase discount tickets that way. For example, General Motors employees get a great discount on Disney tickets because of the company's sponsorship of the Test Track attraction at Epcot.

Disney Ticket Prices and Options

As you may have guessed, nothing is cheap about Walt Disney World. If you're going, you are going to have to spend some money. Disney does their part by providing gorgeous theme parks, outstanding service, and a magical experience every second you are on their property. Disney does it like no other place on Earth, and that level of excellence comes with a price. Park ticket prices are certainly no exception to the rule. The great thing about Disney is they have many ticket options to fit any (well almost any) budget- AND the longer you stay, the cheaper it gets!

Unless you're planning to visit other Orlando area attractions such as Sea World and Universal Orlando, or planning to venture to some of the more distant Florida vacation destinations such as Cape Canaveral or Busch Gardens, a good rule of thumb is to purchase tickets for two to three days fewer than your entire stay. This will help you avoid paying for a full day at the Disney World theme parks on the days you're traveling to and from Orlando. Purchasing tickets for three days fewer than your entire trip will allow for a 'rest day' in the middle of your vacation- which you'll probably really need!

Keep in mind that Disney ticket pricing is geared toward encouraging you to purchase more days. As the number of days increases, the price per day decreases. For example, a 7-day base ticket for an adult (ages 10 and up) is about $12 cheaper per day than the same 5-day ticket. This means you'll get two extra days for just a few dollars more per ticket.

Below is a look at Disney's published prices (in U.S. dollars) for Disney Magic Your Way (base) tickets as of this writing. (Prices listed do not include Florida's 6.5% sales tax.)

Number of Days	Price Per Day		Total Price	
	Ages 10+	Ages 3-9	Ages 10+	Ages 3-9
1	$94.00**	$88.00**	$94.00	$88.00
2	$94.00	$87.50	$188.00	$175.00
3	$91.34	$85.00	$274.00	$255.00
4	$73.50	$68.50	$294.00	$274.00
5	$60.80	$56.80	$304.00	$284.00
6	$52.34	$49.00	$314.00	$294.00
7	$46.29	$43.43	$324.00	$304.00
8	$41.75	$39.25	$334.00	$314.00
9	$38.23	$36.00	$344.00	$324.00
10	$35.40	$3.40	$354.00	$334.00

** Single day prices shown are for Epcot, Animal Kingdom, and Hollywod Studios. Magic Kingdom single day tickets are $5 more.

As you can see from the chart, the longer you stay the cheaper it gets! Three days is the breaking point for the better deal. If you're going to visit Disney for three days, you might as well go for four days because the extra day is only $20! If you're staying longer, it's even better! Extra days after that are only $10 per day!

Disney also has a few other ticket options too. Here's a look at the details for all three:

Magic Your Way

This is the base Disney ticket for admission to any of the four Walt Disney World theme parks. Magic Your Way allows you to visit one park per day for the balance of the number of days purchased. The days do not have to be consecutive, but unless you purchase the "no expiration" option, your tickets will expire 14 days after their first use.

Park Hopper

Disney's Park Hopper option gives visitors the option to visit more than one of the major theme parks at Walt Disney World on the same day. Without a Park Hopper ticket, you must choose between Magic Kingdom, Animal Kingdom, Epcot, and Hollywood Studios on any given day. You can't visit multiple parks on the same day.

The park hopper option is great for families on the go, and for those with older kids that have either been to Walt Disney World before, or who would grow bored if they were to stay at one park for the entire day. Plus, the Extra Magic Hours you're allowed if you're staying at a Disney resort will help you get the most of your day when selecting the Park Hopper option. You can take the monorail between some of the parks, or board a Disney bus for transportation between parks.

If your family is on their first visit to Walt Disney World, or if you have small children, you should probably avoid the park hopper option because you may not be getting your money's worth. First time visitors will enjoy a full day's worth of rides and attractions at any of the parks without feeling the need to venture to another park on the same day. Younger kids will probably not have the stamina to make it through a full day at any of the parks anyway, so you should probably avoid the Park Hopper option if you don't think the kiddies will last.

The cost to add the Park Hopper option to your ticket ranges from $6 per day for a 10-day ticket, up to $35 to add the option to a one-day ticket.

Water Park Fun & More

This is our favorite option! The only time we don't add this option to our tickets is when we visit in December or January. During those months the weather isn't quite as hot, so we don't feel we'd get our money's worth. Plus, this is the prime time for maintenance to be done on the water parks so you may miss out on some attractions.

There are a variety of Disney ticket options

Adding the Water Park Fun & More option to your Disney Magic Your Way ticket will give you the chance to enjoy admission to other exciting attractions at the Walt Disney World Resort. You'll get to visit Disney's awesome water parks, Typhoon Lagoon and Blizzard Beach, plus you can go to Disney's DisneyQuest Indoor Interactive Theme Park. If that's not enough, you'll have the option to visit Disney's Wide World of Sports Complex or play a round of golf at Disney's Oak Trail Golf Course- a relaxed, nine-hole course designed for the entire family, or you can play a round of miniature golf (prior to 4:00 PM) at Disney's Fantasia Gardens or Winter Summerland miniature golf courses.

You'll get one visit to any of these attractions for each day on your Disney ticket. That means a 7-day pass will include seven visits to these cool attractions. You can even visit more than one in a day. For example, you may want to take a break from the major parks and visit a water park in the morning and DisneyQuest (at Downtown Disney) in the evening. Or, play a quick round of golf in the morning (before it gets too hot) then hit Blizzard Beach after lunch!

DisneyQuest at Downtown Disney

The cost to add the Water Park Fun & More option to your Disney tickets ranges from just $6 a day for a 10-day ticket, up to $55 per day to add the option to a one-day ticket.

Why not both?

You can add either Park Hopper or Water Park Fun & More to your Disney Magic Your Way base tickets, or you can get an even better deal and add both options! Although adding both options to a single day ticket is a bit pricey at $81.00, a 10-day adult ticket with both Park Hopper **and**

Water Park Fun & More is only an extra $8.60 per day over and above the cost of your base ticket. Not a bad deal at all!

Let's do the math

The table near the beginning of this section, and the summary of the various ticket options provide the details you need to calculate how much tickets will be for your family for your entire Disney vacation. Here are a couple of scenarios that will help you get a better idea of the total cost of admission you could expect to pay for your family when you visit the parks:

Scenario 1: Family of four, 4-day 'Magic Your Way' base tickets		Scenario 2: Family of four (all ages 10 and up), 7-day tickets with Park Hopper and Water Park Fun & More	
Adult tickets:	$588.00	Adult tickets:	$1,296.00
Kid tickets	$548.00	Park Hopper/Water Park	
Subtotal:	$1,136.00	add-on (4@ $86/each):	$344.00
Florida sales tax:	$73.84	Subtotal:	$1,640.00
		Florida sales tax:	$106.60
Ticket total:	$1,209.84	Ticket total:	$1,746.60

Of course every family is different, so ticket prices, options, and the size of your family will substantially change the total amount you'll spend on tickets, but this gives you an idea. A Disney vacation is quite an investment as you can see. Even a family of four on a short stay with only the base ticket will spend well over $1,000 just to walk into the parks. Just remember, the longer you stay the cheaper it is per day. Also, don't just jump into Park Hopper and the water parks options unless you think you'll use them. One year we added the Park Hopper and only ended up 'hopping' a couple of days so I don't think it was worth it for us that time. Think about your family, how you travel, the ages of your children, and even the time of year you'll be traveling. All of these, along with of course your budget, should be factors in your decision.

Understanding Disney's FastPass+ System

Disney has always had a great system to help you get on the rides faster instead of wasting your time standing in line all day. While many other theme parks add an additional 'up charge' to their tickets of about ½ the price of the regular park admission ticket for those who don't want to wait in line for two hours to get on top attractions (ahem... UNIVERSAL), Disney has never- and hopefully will never do this. Over the course of many years, Disney, always known for their great customer service, perfected their paper ride reservation system called FASTPASS®. (Not using caps for emphasis here- that's the way Disney trademarked it.) FASTPASS was available for the most popular rides and attractions at all four Disney theme parks. The paper process was fairly simple. Instead of going to the regular ride entrance you headed to the area near the entrance where you would find the FASTPASS distribution kiosks. You would put your park ticket into the FASTPASS machine and it would print out your FASTPASS ticket.

Your ride times would be printed on the ticket, as would the time that you would be eligible to obtain your next FASTPASS. Rather than being a specific 'reservation' time, you were given a one hour window to return which provided you some flexibility as you planned your day. Instead of waiting in line for an hour or two, you would be free to walk around the park and enjoy some of the other attractions. You would just come back to the attraction during the timeframe printed on your pass. Instead of getting into the regular line, you proceeded to the FASTPASS Return line and pretty much walk right on! While there was usually a very short wait (mainly the time it takes to walk through the queues), compared to the lines of a couple of hours (or more) at the major attractions during peak times, FASTPASS was a boon for customer service and satisfaction, and always FREE!

Disney's classic paper FASTPASS® system is now a thing of the past

Over the years of increasing attendance at all of Disney's parks, the system began to get a bit overwhelmed. As anyone who has ever gone to Hollywood Studios in the afternoon during peak seasons in the hopes of grabbing a Toy Story Midway Mania FASTPASS will attest, it got to the point that the paper system just didn't work anymore. It was then that Disney decided to scrap the paper FASTPASS system and replace it with the 'new and improved' FastPass+.

FastPass+ takes the original paper system to an all-new level. Gone are the separate paper ticket machines at the prime attractions at each of the parks. Those have been replaced by a limited number of walk-up electronic kiosks at each park, and the new My Disney Experience planner and mobile app. With FastPass+, you can reserve your attractions up to 30 days prior to your Disney vacation, and up to 60 days in advance if you're staying on Disney property.

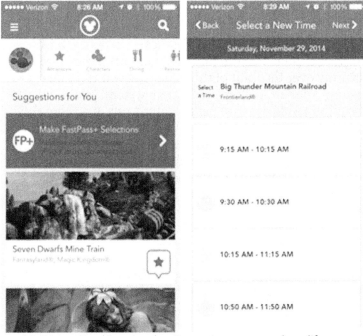

My Disney Experience makes it easy to reserve and modify your FastPass+ reservations

When you purchase your Disney tickets, you simply link them to your account so you can choose your FastPass+ attractions. When you login to the My Disney Experience app or to your account from the Disney site, you'll be able to pick up to three FastPass+ attractions per day at a single park. This gives you the advantage of being able to plan your day in advance based on which park you plan to attend, and what time of day you wish to ride. This can be a disadvantage too for the exact same reason. Some people don't want to plan that far in advance- and you may not even want to plan this way the same day you're attending the park. Don't worry though- if you want to change your plans you can do so the same day. Using the free My Disney Experience smart phone app, or one of the FastPass+ kiosks inside each of the parks, you can even change your attractions right up to the minute you're supposed to ride!

When Disney first launched FastPass+ in pilot mode in 2013, and later with the full launch in 2014, they faced scrutiny over the limit of three FastPass+ attractions per visitor. After all, with the old paper system, you could get an unlimited number of passes- albeit one at a time. How was this an improvement? Furthermore, the limitation of the new system to only allow guests to reserve their FastPass+ attractions at a single park, greatly reduced the benefits of the Park Hopper add-on to the standard Magic Your Way ticket option. Many guests lamented this fact both in person at the parks, and on the Internet. Shortly thereafter, Disney announced enhancements to the system to address those concerns.

Although you can still only reserve three attractions per day in advance, and they can still only be at one park, you are now able to add additional FastPass+'s after your initial passes are used (or have expired) by visiting the kiosks within the parks. (As of this writing you cannot add them using the My Disney Experience app, although I suspect this functionality will be added to the app in a future release.) Also, if you have the Park Hopper option, you can use your pre-reserved passes at one park then hop over to another to visit a kiosk at the new park to reserve your next pass. Once you've used that pass, you can again visit a kiosk to reserve another (and so on, and so on...)

Of course, as with the old system this is still subject to availability. Don't expect to use your passes at Magic Kingdom for example, then hop on over to Hollywood Studios in the early evening during peak season and expect to pick up a FastPass+ for Toy Story Midway Mania. It's not going to happen! Still, it's great to know that after you've used your passes at one park, you at least have a chance to get more- either at the original park or at the one you've 'hopped' to.

FastPass+ was made for rides like Toy Story Midway Mania

FastPass+ tips

- Since you can't obtain more FassPass+'s until after you've used your initial three, it's best to get them as early in the day as possible when reserving them in advance with the My Disney Experience app. It increases the chances that there will be passes left for the top attractions when you reserve your 'add on' passes at the park kiosks.
- Because the passes are in groups in the My Disney Experience app, you won't be able to pick any three attractions in the park. You'll need to pick from an attraction in each group so you won't necessarily get to select all of your favorites.

- Use the My Disney Experience app to check out the wait times for the most popular attractions in advance. That may help you choose your selections.

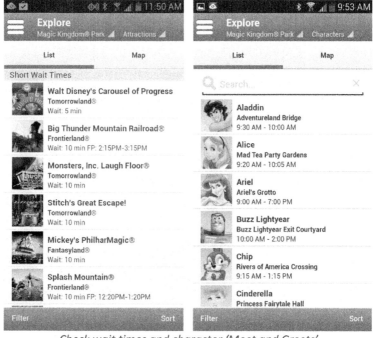

Check wait times and character 'Meet and Greets' with the My Disney Experience app

- Reserve your attractions as soon as you get your tickets, or as soon as you're eligible if you purchase your tickets far in advance. Remember- 30 days in advance if you're staying off of Disney property, and 60 days in advance if you're staying at a Disney resort. You'll get the best times that way, with the most flexibility in your planning, plus you can always change them if your plans change.
- The My Disney Experience app will suggest times for you, but don't feel like you need to take the suggestions. You have the freedom to choose other attractions and times.

4) Orlando Resorts, Hotels, & Other Accommodations

A big portion of the total expense of your Walt Disney World vacation will be your hotel room, condo, or other accommodations in the Orlando area. For some people, their hotel is just a place to sleep. Much of their day is spent in the Disney theme parks and other attractions in the Orlando area. For those people, it's hard to justify spending big bucks on a hotel room regardless of whether or not it's on Disney property.

Other families (like ours) like to have a place to relax and unwind during the morning and evening hours- and maybe even during a mid-day break from the rides and attractions of Disney's theme parks. This type of family can justify spending a bit more for more space, more luxurious accommodations, or even the atmosphere found at higher-end resorts, condominiums, or rental homes.

Topics in this section will provide options and top picks for any budget. Check out the hotel categories topic to see exactly what you'll be getting in each hotel category if you stay on Disney property. You'll find my top picks for Disney deluxe resorts, moderate resorts, value resorts, and deluxe villas. If you plan to stay offsite, I'll examine options for other hotels, condos, and other off-property resorts in the Orlando area- all within a short drive of the Disney theme parks.

Disney World Resort Categories

Disney classifies their resorts according to the size of the rooms, the level of amenities you can expect to receive and the price you'll be asked to pay. Resorts with monorail stops, or those offering boat transportation to one or more of the parks tend to be more expensive than resorts offering only bus service, and those with a more upscale appeal will (of course) be priced at a premium.

Some Disney Deluxe Resorts offer monorail transportation

Here's a look at the categories of Disney resorts and some of the amenities and other features you can expect to find at each level.

Note about room rates: Prices quoted in this section are current at the time of this writing. Unless otherwise noted, they represent weekday rates for standard rooms during the 'regular' season at Disney. Prices vary greatly depending on the time of year, and each location offers a variety of room types. Disney also frequently runs discount specials of up to 30% off of their published rates at various times of the year. These prices are to be used as a general guide. Check the Disney site for current rates, and for any upcoming special offers.

Disney Deluxe Resorts

Here is what you can expect if you choose to stay at a deluxe Disney resort:

- High-end resorts with premium pricing
- Largest rooms with upscale amenities and luxurious decor
- Most deluxe resorts offer convenient transportation to theme parks via a short walk, monorail, or boat
- Most rooms accommodate up to 5 people
- All have table service restaurants and room service available
- Most offer amenities such as a beach area and/or playground, a health club, kids' activities and programs, refrigerators, and babysitting services

The Grand Floridian – A deluxe Disney resort

Disney Moderate Resorts

If you select a Disney moderate resort, here is what you can expect:

- Room sizes comparable to Disney deluxe resorts at greatly reduced prices
- Most rooms accommodate up to five people
- Fewer amenities available than deluxe resorts
- All have table service restaurants and limited room service albeit with fewer options than deluxe resorts
- Transportation to parks is limited to bus service

- All Disney moderate resorts have a playground, marina, and babysitting services
- Other amenities are sparse

Disney Value Reports

- Newest Disney hotel option makes staying on-property affordable for most families
- Most are limited to four guests per room
- No table-service restaurants, but counter service dining options are available
- Smaller no-frills rooms, but hotels are decorated in unique themes
- Transportation to parks limited to bus service
- Value resorts are generally farther away from the parks meaning longer commutes
- All offer pizza-only room service and all have a playground
- There may be an additional charge to rent a refrigerator

Disney Deluxe Villas

- Offer vast array of room types to support larger groups, longer stays, and special needs
- Range from campground to large, luxurious multi-bedroom suites
- Accommodations range from 4 to 12 guests
- All have refrigerators and kitchens or kitchenettes
- All offer bus service to the parks, most offer boat service to the parks
- Most have table-service restaurants, room service, high-speed Internet access and other deluxe amenities
- All have playgrounds and babysitting services, all except one have a health club

Deluxe villas are a great option for families needing extra space

Disney Deluxe Resorts Top Picks

If you decide to stay on Disney property at one of their deluxe resorts, here's a look at a variety of options.

Disney's Yacht Club Resort and Beach Club Resort

Although technically two separate resorts, Disney's Yacht Club and Beach Club Resorts are like two resorts in one. Located in the Epcot area of Walt Disney World, a short walk from the Yacht Club or Beach Club resorts will get you to both Disney's Epcot theme park, and the Disney Boardwalk. You can also take the path from the Yacht and Beach Clubs to Hollywood Studios, but it's a bit longer commute. In addition, you can take water transportation to both Epcot and Hollywood Studios. As with all Disney resorts, you can also use the Disney bus service for transportation to and from the other parks and Downtown Disney.

The pool is shared by these two resorts, and it is just gorgeous! A river winds throughout the complex, creating a number of private areas. This layout is much more scenic and cozy than having one big pool in a wide-open space. Disney's Yacht Club and Beach Club Resorts are also home to Stormalong Bay- their very own water park!

Although Disney's Yacht Club Resort and Beach Club Resort share many of the same amenities and facilities, the decor of the two hotels gives them a unique feel. The Yacht Club is representative of an upper-class east coast harbor club whereas the Beach Club Resort straddles the middle ground between formal and fun.

Disney Beach Club Resort

Rooms at these two deluxe Disney resorts can accommodate up to four or five guests, and range in price from around $400-$600 per night depending on the room and season. Both resorts also offer club level two-bedroom suites that range from $1,600-$1,800 per night during peak seasons. Definitely on the pricey side, but if you can afford the cost of admission, these two resorts will aid in making your Disney stay a truly magical and memorable experience!

Disney's Animal Kingdom Lodge

Disney's Animal Kingdom Lodge is truly a unique experience that will make you feel as if you're on an African safari! Located in the Animal Kingdom area of Walt Disney World, this deluxe resort is bordered by wildlife areas that will enable hotel guests to observe and enjoy wildlife from various viewing areas throughout the resort. Many rooms actually overlook the savannah allowing you to watch zebras, giraffes and other animals roaming from the comfort of your own balcony!

The hotel is decorated in an African motif including African art, colorful tribal masks, and other artifacts. Guides are available to talk to guests and answer questions regarding the many species of wildlife at the resort. Like the rooms at Disney's Yacht Club and Beach Club resorts, rooms at Disney's Animal Kingdom Lodge can accommodate 4 or 5 guests. Prices for standard rooms here are a bit cheaper than those at the Yacht Club and Beach

Club resorts, ranging from the mid $300s to around $500 per night depending on the season. Similar to the offerings at both the Yacht and Beach Club resorts, you also have the option to upgrade to one or two-bedroom club level suites at Animal Kingdom. Pricing for those is a bit less than the suites at the Yacht and Beach Clubs topping off at just over $1,600 per night for the two-bedroom option.

Savannah view rooms at Disney's Animal Kingdom Lodge

Disney's Animal Kingdom Lodge also offers deluxe villa options in the Jambo House and Kidani Village sections of the resort.

Disney Boardwalk Inn

Disney's Boardwalk Inn became our favorite Disney resort from nearly the moment we walked in during our recent stay. Of course some of this *may* have had to do with the fact that we were selected as Boardwalk Inn's "Family of the Day" when we checked in, but even if we weren't bestowed that honor and showered with fabulous prizes, I'm sure we would have loved the resort anyway- it's just a really fun place to be! (Truth be told- the 'fabulous prizes' amounted to a balloon bouquet, a certificate, a photo, and a free surrey bike rental, but hey- it's sometimes the little touches that make things special!)

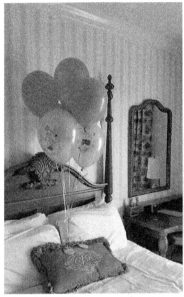

A room and a view at Disney's Boardwalk Inn

From the moment you approach Disney's Boardwalk Inn, you'll realize it's not quite like any other Disney resort. You'll experience the whimsy and charm of turn-of-the-century Atlantic City complete with a boardwalk (of course!), a carousel, and a roller coaster (sort of).

As you walk through the doors at the Boardwalk, you'll be greeted by an opulent lobby with a beautiful model carousel. While you're there, check out the highly detailed roller coaster model- an exact replica of a period-authentic coaster on Atlantic City's boardwalk. As you head out toward the main pool and boardwalk area, you'll see another giant coaster. However, this one is really a super-fun water slide! While the rooms and facilities at Disney's Boardwalk Inn are second to none, this area- the outdoor boardwalk area is where Disney's Boardwalk Inn really shines!

Period-authentic roller coaster & carousel models

Located on the shores of Crescent Lake, nestled between Epcot and Hollywood Studios, Disney's boardwalk evokes the feeling of truly being transported to the famous boardwalk in Atlantic City with its array of eateries, street performers, and quaint shops. Keep an eye out for the surrey bikes that are sure to be making the trek around the lake. Take a stroll around the lake to check out Disney's Yacht and Beach club on the other side, or wander over to the Swan & Dolphin hotels which are just a short walk away. If you're looking for a little nightlife, leave the kids at the pool and head on over to the Jellyrolls bar for a little dueling pianos action. Day or night you'll find an abundance of activity around the boardwalk- that's what makes it the place to be!

Another great perk of staying at Disney's Boardwalk Inn is its proximity to both Disney's Hollywood Studios and

Epcot theme parks. It's a short boat ride to both parks, and both are even close enough to reach on foot. Much more convenient than needing to catch a bus each and every time you head out to the parks.

Disney's Boardwalk comes alive at night!

Rooms at Disney's Boardwalk Inn range from the low $400's for a non-discounted standard room during the summer season up to about $800 for a deluxe club level room. There are also deluxe studio and one and two-bedroom villas available in a similar price range.

The lobby at Disney's Boardwalk Inn

Disney's Polynesian Village Resort

If you're looking for a great on-property hotel for your stay at Walt Disney World, and a deluxe resort is within your budget, you should definitely check out (and check-in to) Disney's Polynesian Village Resort.

The Polynesian is one of Disney's original resort hotels (the other is the Contemporary resort) that have been around since the opening of the Magic Kingdom theme park way back in 1971. It is one of four Disney resorts offering monorail transportation to the Magic Kingdom and Epcot theme parks, which is a great convenience for guests during their stay. Disney's Grand Floridian, Contemporary Resort, and Bay Lake Tower offer a similar convenience.

The lush tropical grounds at Disney's Polynesian Resort Village

The Polynesian Village resort consists of several separate buildings with names like 'Tahiti', 'Hawaii', 'Samoa', and 'Tokelau', authentically presented with 'island flair', a couple of pools (including one with a giant volcano and water slide), and a variety of restaurants and gift shops to explore and enjoy. The lush tropical grounds feature two pools, and can be traversed using a variety of winding pathways through the gorgeous tropical foliage. There are several small waterfalls and creeks dotting the landscape which provide a truly immersive experience for you to enjoy.

The volcano water slide promises a hot time for the entire family

The centerpiece of the resort is the Great Ceremonial House which is the lobby of the resort and contains the resort's restaurants and gift shops. It is also home to a very nice little arcade for the videogame buffs in the family.

The Polynesian's three restaurants are 'Ohana, Captain Cook's, and Kona Café. 'Ohana features a delicious family-style all-you-can-eat feast of skewers and skewers of beef, pork, and shrimp cooked over an open wood burning grill and topped off with a variety of delicious side dishes. There is also a character breakfast available each morning at 'Ohana featuring Mickey and Pluto. Captain Cook's is a quick-service restaurant offering both standard American dishes and authentic Polynesian offerings throughout the day, and Kona Café is a sit-down dining experience offering dishes such as Tonga Toast and Macadamia Pineapple Pancakes for breakfast, Big Island Tacos and an Island Chicken Sandwich for lunch, and Grilled Lamb Chops and Togarashi Spiced Ahi Tuna for dinner.

As you're touring the grounds, be sure to make a reservation at 'Ohana

The resort has a beautiful beach on the shores of the Seven Seas Lagoon that looks out toward the Magic Kingdom and Cinderella Castle towering in the distance. There are nightly movies on the beach as well as an Electrical Water Pageant light show in the lagoon each evening. Each evening you can enjoy the "Wishes" fireworks extravaganza from the beach or from the comfort of your balcony if you've upgraded to a room with a 'Theme Park view'. If you want to get fully immersed in the tastes, sights, and sounds of the islands, you can also check out the Spirit of Aloha dinner show and luau occurring twice each evening. The luau requires a separate ticket (which includes dinner) that runs about $60-$75 depending on where you sit, but it's a pretty cool event if you're willing to invest the time and money.

Room rates at Disney's Polynesian Village Resort during Disney's peak season range from around $500 for a standard view room up to about $900 for a club level room with a theme park view. If you're looking for luxury resort on the monorail route, Disney's Polynesian Village Resort should definitely be on your short list of Disney resorts.

Other Disney Deluxe Resorts

Here's a listing of other Disney Deluxe Resorts:

- Disney's Contemporary Resort
- Disney's Grand Floridian Resort & Spa
- Disney's Wilderness Lodge

Disney's Contemporary Resort (left) & The Grand Floridian

Disney Moderate Resorts

If Disney's deluxe resorts are out of your price range, you may want to consider one of Disney's moderate resorts instead. These resorts offer many of the amenities you'll find at the deluxe resorts, but are a bit less expensive. Some of the moderate resorts only allow a maximum of four guests per room, so if you're a family of five, your options will be limited. Here's a look at a couple of options:

Disney's Port Orleans Resort – French Quarter

Disney's Port Orleans Resort – French Quarter is like a trip to the Big Easy, and home of the Mardi Gras- New Orleans. Located in the Downtown Disney area of Walt Disney World, this version of Bourbon Street is much more family-oriented and laid-back than the original and features plenty of open space to allow you to unwind after a long day of touring the Disney theme parks.

Day or night, the charm shines bright at French Quarter

Disney's Port Orleans French Quarter is the smallest of Disney's moderate resorts, and also one of the most popular. The resort's 1000+ rooms are split amongst seven buildings situated along the quaint streets of the 'Quarter.

The hotel interior and architecture reflects that of the Deep South, and the staff will provide a healthy dose of southern hospitality. Boat transportation is available to Downtown Disney, and buses will take you to all of the Disney theme parks and water parks.

Rooms at the French Quarter are simple yet elegant

Rooms are modestly equipped, expectedly lacking some of the elegance and pizzazz of the rooms at Walt Disney World's deluxe resorts, and accommodate a maximum of four guests. Families of five should consider Disney's Port Orleans Resort – Riverside just across the Sassagoula River instead. Riverside offers accommodations for up to five guests. If you have a family of four, Disney's Port Orleans Resort – French Quarter is a great option. Rooms here are much cheaper than some of the other moderate resorts, available at a nightly rate in the low $200s.

Disney's Caribbean Beach Resort

Located in the Epcot area of Walt Disney World, Disney's Caribbean Beach Resort is the most centrally located of all of Disney's moderate resorts. This means you'll spend less time on buses getting to the theme parks, water parks, and Downtown Disney than at some of the other moderate hotels. However, since the resort is huge, you'll spend a fair amount of time aboard the bus, stopping at the various stops within the resort, before you even leave the resort to head for the parks. At the Caribbean Beach, you'll also find the largest rooms of any of Disney's moderate resorts.

The entrance to Disney's Caribbean Beach Resort

The buildings of the resort are arranged in several small groups surrounding a lake. Rooms at Disney's Caribbean Beach Resort range in price from about $180 to $235, with the nicer rooms having views of the lakes located around the resort. The atmosphere at the Caribbean Beach Resort is (of course) designed to resemble that of one of the many beautiful islands in the Caribbean Sea. Each section of the resort is named after a Caribbean island so if you stay here and explore the resort, you'll be able to tell your friends that you visited tropical locales such as Barbados, Aruba, and Martinique when you get back from your central Florida vacation!

The brightly colored buildings and laid back atmosphere lend to the Caribbean ambiance. Rather than one large pool, Disney's Caribbean Beach Resort features several smaller pools which makes each pool seem less crowded.

One of the pools at Disney's Caribbean Beach Resort

Other moderate Disney resorts

The rest of Disney's moderate resorts include:

- Disney's Coronado Springs Resort
- The Cabins at Disney's Fort Wilderness Resort
- Disney's Port Orleans Resort - Riverside

Disney Value Resorts

If you're traveling on a budget but still want to enjoy staying on-property at Walt Disney World, consider one of Disney's Value Resorts. You'll still get (most of) the Disney experience without many of the amenities available at the other resorts.

Here's a look at a couple of options:

Disney's Pop Century Resort

Located in Disney's Epcot area, Disney's Pop Century Resort is one of the newer value resorts at Walt Disney World. Each value resort at Disney is decorated in a unique theme, faithfully carried out throughout the resort. Disney's Pop Century Resort is like taking a journey through 50 years of American pop culture. A maximum of four guests per room are allowed at Disney's Pop Century Resort (as well as Disney's All Star Sports Resort and Disney's All-Star Movies Resort), so families of five on a tight budget will have only Disney's Art of Animation and Disney's All-Star Music Resort as available options in the value resort category.

Disney's Pop Century Resort

Rooms at Pop Century range from around $150 to $175 per night during the summer season. The rooms are very small with two double beds and not much else in the room. If you're looking for action and excitement, try to get a room near the playground or pool areas. If you're looking for a quieter setting, request a room overlooking the lake at this resort.

This sprawling Disney value resort has a building dedicated to each decade from the 1950s to the 1990s. The décor in each building faithfully represents the appropriate decade. This makes it quite fun to check out the different buildings- all unique in their own way. Stroll through the 1950s section and you'll be greeted by bowling pin staircases, 45 rpm records (remember those?) and a Lady and the Tramp statue.

In the 60s you'll find yo-yos, Play-Doh and plenty of peace signs, or be greeted by 8-track tape, Rubik's Cube, or cell phone staircases in the 70s, 80s, and 90s respectively. The sheer vastness of the resort means you'll want to save some time to explore each of the sections as you journey through American pop culture. Because of the size of the complex, you may have quite a walk to get to the bus stop to board the Disney busses that will take you to the four major theme parks, Typhoon Lagoon and Blizzard Beach water parks, and to Downtown Disney.

As with all Disney Value Resorts, Disney's Pop Century resort does not offer any sit-down restaurants. Dining options include quick-service dining at the Everything POP

Shopping & Dining food court, the Petals pool bar, and in-room pizza delivery.

Disney's All Star Sports Resort

The main entrance at Disney's All-Star Sports Resort

It there's a sports fan in your family, and you're looking to stay on-property at one of Walt Disney World's value resorts, then Disney's All-Star Sports Resort may be just the ticket to a slam dunk vacation. Located in the Animal Kingdom area of Walt Disney World, Disney's All-Star

Sports Resort is true to its name with the sports theme carried throughout.

Halls in the resort are named after sports such a surfing, football, basketball, and tennis. You'll even find a three-story-high football helmet and 30 foot basketball hoops! The surfing hall is one of the prime locations in the hotel. The side facing away from the pool will be one of the quieter areas in the resort. As with other Disney value resorts, rooms near the playground and pool area will be pretty loud. If you'd like a little peace and quiet at the end of your day, you may want to steer clear of those areas. Depending on your room location, you may have quite a long walk to the bus transportation that takes you to the parks.

Bring your "A" game for a great time at All-Star Sports

Like Disney's other value resorts, Disney's All-Star Sports Resort does not feature any table service restaurants. If you want to eat at the resort, you'll be limited to a food court and room service pizza.

Rooms at Disney's All-Star Sports Resort are small, as expected. You'll be limited to four guests per room and two double beds. Expect to pay around $140-$160 for a room at Disney's All-Star Sports Resort during the summer vacation season. Rooms run about $40 cheaper per night during the value seasons.

Disney's Art of Animation Resort

If you dream of being fully immersed in one of Disney's full-length modern classics such as Finding Nemo, The Lion King, or Cars, Disney's Art of Animation Resort may be just the place for you! The newest (and most awesome!) of Disney's value resorts, Art of Animation consists mostly of family suites designed to sleep up to six adults, so the rooms are a bit pricier than other value resorts. You can expect to pay in the high $300s for a family suite during the summer season. If you're only traveling with a party of four, you can get by with a Little Mermaid standard room for about $170 during the same time of year. Disney's Art of Animation Resort is located right next door to Disney's Pop Century Resort in the Wide World of Sports area of Walt Disney World.

The Finding Nemo section at Art of Animation

If a family suite is what you prefer, you'll have the option of choosing between Cars, The Lion King, or Finding Nemo themes, all exploding with characters and the brightly animated color palettes of each Disney feature film.

The outdoor areas and walkways of the resort are similarly decorated as well. I was especially amazed at the vegetation in the Finding Nemo section. The underwater plants looked like they were plucked right from the film and plopped into the middle of the resort! Very cool! If you have a Cars fan in your family, you'll definitely want to pick that theme and to spend some time taking advantage of the photo ops with Lightning McQueen, Mater, Doc Hudson, or many of your other favorites from the movie.

The Cars section of the resort

If you choose to stay at Disney's Art of Animation Resort, you'll have your choice of three pools including the Finding Nemo themed pool- the largest resort pool in all of Walt Disney World, and two smaller pools for the little ones. Your dining options are similar to those available at Disney's other value resorts and include the Landscape of Flavors food court and in-room pizza delivery.

If you're looking for a Disney value resort that's a cut above the rest, check out Disney's Art of Animation Resort. It's tons of fun for everyone!

The Flippin' Fins Pool is fun for tiny tikes

Other Disney Value Resorts

Here's a look at the remaining Disney Value Resorts:

- Disney's All-Star Movies Resort
- Disney's All-Star Music Resort

Disney Deluxe Villas

If you're looking to vacation in the lap of luxury but need more space than even Disney's deluxe resorts can provide, the deluxe villa option may be right for you. With one and two bedroom villas, and some other unique options available, Disney's deluxe villa option is great for a growing family who needs the space, and can afford the luxury of staying at a high-end Disney resort.

Here's a look at a couple of possibilities should you decide the deluxe villa option is right for you.

Disney's Old Key West Resort

If a taste of the islands is what you seek, Disney's Old Key West Resort might be just the place for you! Located in the Downtown Disney area of Walt Disney World, this quaint resort featuring two and three bedroom bungalows will take you back to turn of the century island life in the Keys with its soft color palate of relaxing pink, blue, and green pastels and lush landscapes with flowering tropical plants and majestic palms. Its proximity to the Downtown Disney area means it's just a short boat ride to Disney's premier shopping and entertainment area.

Old Key West is just a short boat ride from Downtown Disney

The resort features four pools including the main 149,000 gallon pool that is home to a sweeping, twisting, turning sandcastle water slide and sandy beach. As a member of Disney's deluxe resort family, Old Key West also features amenities such as a playground, jogging trail, and a full array of sports options including basketball, volleyball, and tennis. There are also bicycle and surrey bike rentals available.

During your stay, be sure to stop by Olivia's café located near the main pool at the front of the resort. Olivia's features a variety of traditional American cuisine options and Island-inspired dishes, and is decorated in a beautiful nautical theme. Non-discounted rooms range from the mid-$300s per night for a deluxe studio, up to around $750 for a two-bedroom villa.

Master bath and bedroom

One-bedroom villa kitchen

The Villas at Disney's Wilderness Lodge

If you're looking to take a journey to the wild west of the late 1800s, look no further than The Villas at Disney's Wilderness Lodge. The lodge resembles a railroad hotel from the days of the American Wild West and offers all the comforts of home while throwing in some unique rustic charm.

The Lobby at Disney's Wilderness Lodge

If you've ever visited the Old Faithful Inn at Wyoming's Yellowstone National Park, you'll have a feeling of déjà vu when you enter the lobby at Disney's Wilderness Lodge. The soaring ceiling and rustic features will have you wondering if you've truly been transported out west. You'll be in awe as you encounter the massive stone fireplace surrounded by wooden rocking chairs. The illusion will come full circle when you explore the grounds and are greeted by volcanic geysers and beautifully landscaped hot springs in the Silver Creek Springs pool area.

Like other Disney deluxe villa resorts, you'll have a variety of dining options during your stay at Wilderness Lodge. Enjoy a fine dining experience in rustic elegance at Artist Point featuring Pacific Northwest fare such as cedar plank roasted king salmon, Applewood smoked Cornish hen, and hickory char-crusted filet mignon. If you're seeking a less formal experience, check out the Whispering Canyon Café, or any of the quick service offerings available at the Roaring Fork or Trout Pass Pool Bar. The resort is also home to the Territory Lounge featuring northwestern wines and craft beers for those wishing to relax with an evening cocktail.

Silver Creek Springs

Rooms at The Villas at Disney's Wilderness Lodge range from the low $400s for a deluxe studio during peak season to just over $1,000 per night for a two-bedroom villa that sleeps up to eight adults.

Other Disney Deluxe Villa Resorts

- Animal Kingdom Jambo House & Kidani Village
- Bay Lake Tower at Disney's Contemporary Resort
- Disney's Beach Club Villas
- Disney's Boardwalk Villas
- Disney's Treehouse Villas
- The Villas at Disney's Grand Floridian Resort & Spa
- Disney's Saratoga Springs Resort & Spa

Staying Off Disney Property

If none of the Disney resorts pique your interest, or perhaps if the ones you're interested in are not quite within your budget, you may decide to stay off-property instead. If you decide to stay off of Disney property, you'll give up some of the perks offered to those who stay at Disney's resorts. You won't have the option of taking Disney's Magical Express shuttle service, and Disney won't deliver your luggage to your hotel. You also won't be able to utilize Extra Magic Hours offered at select parks on various days throughout the week, and you don't qualify for the Disney dining plan. Another perk you'll lose by staying off-property is the ability to book your FastPass+ and dining reservations as far in advance as those staying at Disney resorts.

Still, after reviewing the Disney hotels in the various Disney World resort categories, you may decide that staying offsite is the best option for your family. As I mentioned in the introduction, I am not one of those authors that will tell you that you absolutely, positively should stay at a Disney resort. We have had many great Disney vacations staying off-property. You just need to make some adjustments to when and how you do things, and you will face some limitations with regard to dining reservations, etc. Still, you may want to stay off property because...

- The thought of staying in a 450 sq. foot room at one of Disney's Value resorts with few of the 'conveniences of home' doesn't appeal to you.
- You can't afford the $300-$500+ per night to stay at some of Disney's moderate or luxury offerings.
- You have three (or more) kids, and the Disney hotels that can accommodate your family do not appeal to you, or are not within your budget.

- You want to visit some of the other Central Florida attractions, and you want your own transportation.

Whatever the reason, you're in luck because the Orlando area has plenty of options for hotels, condominiums, and rental homes for every budget.

Which location is best?

You'll find numerous options for hotels, condos, and rental homes within a 20 minute drive of the major theme parks of Walt Disney World. There are three main areas in the region where you'll find the best options: Exits 62 and 68 off of I-4, and also the abundance of hotels and other accommodations off of International Drive in the Lake Buena Vista, Kissimmee, and Orlando areas.

There are many options for accommodations in the Orlando area

Exit 68 off of I-4 is the closest of the three hotel and restaurant areas to the Walt Disney World theme parks. There are a variety of hotel chains and restaurants within a 10-20 minute drive of the Disney parks. One thing I'll point out is that in certain areas you'll be challenged by some traffic bottlenecks that will make your drive longer. Exit 62 is a bit farther out, but still a short drive to the theme parks. The added distance means you'll save $20-$30 per night for similar accommodations when compared with the prices you'll pay for the hotels at exit 68.

A little further out, but still within a 20 minute drive of the Disney theme parks is International Drive. Hotels and accommodations in this area are a bit cheaper than those at the two I-4 exits, and you'll have the added benefit of being closer to SeaWorld and Universal Orlando. This makes it a great location if you're planning on visiting either or both of these outstanding Orlando vacation destinations.

Other things to consider when staying offsite

Here are some other things to consider when deciding where to stay in the Orlando area:

- See if the hotel offers a free breakfast, and whether it's a full, hot breakfast or just a continental breakfast. A full breakfast can easily save you $10-$15 per person per day.
- See if the hotel offers free shuttle service to the parks. Remember though if your bus is stopping at all the parks, you may have a lengthy commute. You may still want to consider renting a car.
- See if kids stay free, and what age is considered a 'kid'. Ages vary by hotel.
- Can you get a suite with a kitchenette? Or at least a room with a refrigerator? Having a place to keep leftovers, drinks, and snacks cold can save you money in the long run.
- How close is the hotel to Disney parks, area restaurants, and other attractions?
- Try calling the hotel's 800 number, and also directly to the hotel. You may be quoted different prices.

- When you call directly to the hotel or resort, ask specifically if they have a "manager's special" or any other unpublished discounts.
- See if the hotel offers discount tickets to Disney theme parks or other Orlando-area attractions such as Universal Orlando and SeaWorld.
- Check to see if the hotel or resort has partnered with any rental car companies to provide discounted rates for guests. If you're renting a car, this may amount to a substantial savings over the course of a one-week stay.

Orlando area 'best bets'

With so many options for hotels, condos, and rental homes in the Orlando area, it would be impossible to cover even a fraction of them here. Your best strategy when considering these options is to compare price, amenities, and location for each option using one of the many online travel sites available. Consider how much space you'll need, and how much time you may spend at your 'home base'. It may be important for you to have a nice pool, or to get shuttle service to the parks. Check out online reviews to see what others who have stayed thought of their accommodations.

Here are a few resorts and hotels worth a look:

Hyatt Regency Grand Cypress

If you're looking for luxurious accommodations in a great location and you're looking for a place that offers golf, tennis, and swimming (you can even go sailing and horseback riding!) during your Disney 'down time', check out the Hyatt Regency Grand Cypress in Lake Buena Vista, Florida. The Hyatt Regency Grand Cypress is so close to Disney World it's almost as good as staying onsite. In addition, you'll only be a 15 minute drive from Universal Orlando and SeaWorld too!

The main pool at Grand Cypress

The resort's pool area is beautiful, with numerous waterfalls and secluded whirlpools. There are a variety of upscale dining options available including a restaurant atop one of the waterfalls! Kids will find plenty to do at Camp Hyatt, a kids club that features games and activities, poolside movies, tennis lessons, and more.

Standard rooms at the Hyatt Regency Grand Cypress begin in the $130s, with prices for lake view and pool view deluxe rooms running about $100 more.

Gaylord Palms Resort & Spa

Located in Kissimmee, Florida just a few miles from Walt Disney World, the Gaylord Palms Resort & Spa offers luxurious accommodations comparable to Disney's deluxe resorts for a more reasonable price. This hotel is pricier than the Hyatt Regency Grand Cypress with standard rooms starting in the low-$200s during the week and about $100 more on weekends.

The hotel is huge and beautiful, built in the opulent style of a turn-of-the-century Florida mansion and resembling a lakefront castle. You'll get all the amenities you'd expect in a luxury hotel including a spa and fitness center, five restaurants and lounges, and activities such as golf, sand volleyball, and more. The resort also features the Cypress Springs Family Fun Water Park- a beautiful pool area with a water slide, a waterfall, and sandy play areas for the kids.

Cypress Springs Family Fun Water Park

The rooms at the resort are beautifully decorated with fine attention to detail. Plush, custom mattresses will help guarantee a good night sleep so you'll be refreshed and ready to hit the Disney theme parks every day.

Embassy Suites Lake Buena Vista

Embassy Suites hotels have always been a favorite of our family. Their 'all suite' layouts provide a great option for families who like a little extra space, and for moms and dads that need a break from the kids once in a while. The kids enjoy having their own space too!

The Embassy Suites Lake Buena Vista hotel is a very popular choice for families visiting the Orlando area. The suites are well maintained and include kitchenettes. Best of all, a full hot breakfast including made-to-order pancakes and omelets is included in the price! For a family like ours, this is a perk worth more than $50 per day.

Embassy Suites Lake Buena Vista atrium

Of the four Embassy Suites hotels in the Orlando area, the Lake Buena Vista location is the closest to the major theme parks of Walt Disney World. Universal Orlando and SeaWorld are nearby too.

Having a kitchenette in your room is a nice little perk that can also save you money. There's a nearby grocery store so you can stock up on snacks and lunch foods and pack a sandwich for lunch in the parks. Considering the prices at some of the Disney restaurants, this can be a great benefit!

There's a nice indoor-outdoor pool at the hotel, and also a gym, tennis courts, basketball and volleyball. Rooms at the Embassy Suites Lake Buena Vista run about $150.

WorldQuest Resort

Conveniently located off of World Center Drive near the intersection of highways 417 and 535, WorldQuest Resort offers luxurious accommodations and a convenient location at a tremendous value. WorldQuest Resort is an all condo resort offering deluxe two and three-bedroom units at a very competitive price. Each of these units features two full baths to meet the needs of growing families, and the three-bedroom units let you sprawl out over 1,440 square feet of space! You can even upgrade to their Superior three-bedroom suite which offers the same amount of space, but adds a 3rd bath.

All units feature a king bed in the master bedroom and large jetted tub in the master bath. Each also has a full (and fully furnished) kitchen and a giant screened in balcony complete with table and chairs so you can enjoy your morning coffee or an evening snack without worrying about flies, mosquitoes, or other creepy crawlies impeding on your relaxation.

The resort also features a beautifully landscaped pool area with plenty of beach chairs and shady spots should you need to escape the hot Florida sun. You can also visit the Tiki Bar, an outdoor pool bar, for an adult beverage as you relax at the end of your day. The Tiki Bar features abundant shaded seating near the pool.

All units at WorldQuest feature a full kitchen

The pool and grounds of WorldQuest Resort

WorldQuest offers a complimentary continental breakfast to guests each morning. Nothing fancy, just cereals, baked goods, fruit, yogurt and such. Although you could certainly enjoy a hot breakfast in your own rental unit, it's nice to have that quick, convenient option available.

The only downside that I have found with this resort comes as a result of one of its benefits- its location. Being conveniently located near multiple freeways makes it easy to get to Disney parks and nearby Downtown Disney, however it's almost too close to some of Central Florida's main arteries. No matter where you are in the resort, you can expect to hear some freeway noise. You won't notice it much in your suite due to thick walls and a decent amount of soundproofing, but you will definitely notice it as you relax on your balcony. I would frequently sit on the balcony to enjoy my morning coffee, or to relax in the evening after a long day in the parks.

Our unit offered a scenic view- of the freeway

The noise from the road was a bit of a nuisance and I found myself putting in earbuds and using music to drown out the freeway noise. If you don't think this will be an issue for you, by all means, check out WorldQuest Resort. Units run from around $130 in the off season up to around $200 per night during the summer months. The Superior three-bedroom units run about $20 higher. When you consider the amount of space, convenience, and luxury you're getting for your money, WorldQuest Resort in Orlando is one of the best values you'll find on your vacation to Walt Disney World.

Floridays Resort

If the idea of being cramped in a small hotel room with none of the conveniences of home does not appeal to you, and the idea of spending your Disney vacation in a luxurious two or three-bedroom condominium DOES, check out Floridays resort.

Floridays is a great off-property option

Floridays is a condominium resort complex consisting of privately owned units that are rented individually and managed by Paramount Hospitality Management, LLC. The two bedroom units where we've stayed on several of our trips to Disney have fully equipped kitchens, a separate dining area, and a king master-suite with a huge bathroom and a two-person whirlpool! With over 1,100 square feet of living space, you're sure to have plenty of room. You can also upgrade to a three-bedroom unit if you need the extra space. The kids love having their own bedroom with two double-beds and a TV. The unit also features a flat-panel HDTV and DVD player in the living room, and another TV in the master bedroom. All of these conveniences provide a great way to relax after a long day in the hot sun.

Floridays 2-bedroom condo

Floridays resort has two pools- a main pool complete with a poolside lounge and plenty of spray fountains for the kids, and a separate smaller pool for quiet relaxation. The resort is conveniently located near a strip mall with a grocery store and a drug store making it easy to stock up on the necessities you'll need for your stay at Walt Disney World. There are also several great restaurants within a five minute drive of the Floridays resort.

Two-bedroom units at Floridays start around $190 per night during peak seasons, and are slightly less expensive during off-peak times. Three-bedroom units that offer about 1,400 square feet of living space run about $40-$60 more.

5) Walt Disney World Theme Parks

But enough about planning, booking, and thinking about all the things you'll need to do to prepare for your magical journey to Walt Disney World. It's time to talk about the parks, and all the awesome things you'll get to do once you're there!

The four theme parks of Walt Disney World: Magic Kingdom, Epcot, Animal Kingdom, and Hollywood Studios will provide hours upon hours of entertainment for your family. If time permits, be sure to visit them all! If it's within your budget, I'd recommend a 7-day park pass which will allow you to visit each park once, and then return to visit your three favorites again! During most of our Disney vacations, we'll visit Magic Kingdom at least three times, and sometimes we STILL don't get to every attraction that we hope to visit!

You're sure to spend lots of time at Magic Kingdom

To get the complete Disney experience, you'll want to visit all four of the major theme parks, but where you spend the majority of your time will likely depend on the ages of your kids, and your family's interests. Families with younger children (or adults who are still kids at heart) will likely spend the majority of their time at Magic Kingdom. There are tons of great things to do there that will most certainly keep you busy and entertained throughout your stay. As the kids get a little older, you'll gradually find yourself spending more of your time at Hollywood Studios and Epcot, and if you are fans of wildlife, you'll definitely be spending a fair amount of time at Animal Kingdom too.

Magic Kingdom

Magic Kingdom, the original Walt Disney World Theme park, opened in 1971. It was the grand vision of Walt Disney himself. Unfortunately, Walt did not live to see the construction of the park, which began in 1967- nearly a year after his death.

Originally dubbed 'The Florida Project' to keep the cost of acquiring land down as Disney secretly planned the park, Magic Kingdom was modeled after Disneyland in California. The park is based on the classic 'spoke and hub' layout with Cinderella Castle at the center of the wheel- surrounded by the various 'lands' of Magic Kingdom.

If you're like most people, Disney's Magic Kingdom will be the first park you visit on your trip to Disney World, and the one where you'll spend most of your time. Being the first of the Disney World parks, it is still the crown jewel of all the Disney theme parks- with good reason!

From the beginning of the park opening show, to the last explosion of the nightly Wishes fireworks extravaganza, your day at Disney's Magic Kingdom will truly be 'magical'. It's more than just hype, or a marketing gimmick, the Disney staff will do an incredible job of making you feel special throughout the day.

Main Street, U.S.A.

Magic Kingdom is made up of six lands, each with its own unique theme and feel. The lands are: Main Street, U.S.A., Adventureland, Frontierland, Liberty Square, Fantasyland, and Tomorrowland. A seventh land, Mickey's Toontown Fair was closed in 2011 to make room for the expansion of Fantasyland. Like the cast members say in the opening show, Disney is truly the happiest place on earth!

Main Street, U.S.A.

Main Street, U.S.A. is a series of shops arranged in rows beginning at the entrance to the park and ending near Cinderella Castle. The shops' architecture is modeled after early 1900's Victorian-era shops, with merchandise ranging from collectibles to jewelry and traditional souvenirs (T-shirts, hats, etc.). Be sure to stop by the Main

Street Bakery and the Plaza Ice Cream Parlor for some tasty treats! They're located near the end of the street on the right as you walk toward the Castle.

Cinderella Castle at the end of Main Street, U.S.A.

Although Main Street, U.S.A. does not feature any rides or attractions, it is home to City Hall (Guest Relations, Lost & Found), Main Street Chamber of Commerce (Package Pickup), The Town Square Theater, and even a barbershop! Main Street also features Tony's Town Square restaurant which is uniquely themed after Disney's Lady and the Tramp movie. The main station of the Walt Disney World Railroad also boards at the beginning of Main Street, just inside the park gates.

Main Street ends in a 'roundabout' just in front of Cinderella Castle with 'spokes' leading to the rest of the lands of the Magic Kingdom.

Town Square Theater at Magic Kingdom

Adventureland

Turn left near the end of Main Street and you'll be headed toward Adventureland. Adventureland is the perfect place for those seeking exotic adventure. Climb the Swiss Family Robinson Tree House, fly through the air on the Magic Carpets of Aladdin, sail the high seas in Pirates of the Caribbean, and take the Jungle Cruise through exotic landscapes.

Pirates of the Caribbean in Adventureland

Frontierland

Continue on past Adventureland, and you'll be headed for Frontierland! Say "Howdy, partners!" at Disney's version of the Wild West. Located between Adventureland and Liberty Square, Frontierland features attractions such as Tom Sawyer's Island, Big Thunder Mountain Railroad, and the fun-for-all-ages Splash Mountain. Head to the Country Bear Jamboree for some foot stompin', toe-tapping good times, and then stop in at the Frontierland Shootin' Arcade to test your skills.

Liberty Square

Tucked between Frontierland and Fantasyland is Liberty Square. This small area separates Frontierland and Fantasyland. It represents Colonial days in America in a really fun way! Visit the Hall of Presidents, ride the Liberty Belle Riverboat, and scare yourself silly in the Haunted Mansion. (Despite its scary name, this ride is actually quite fun and not too scary.)

The Liberty Belle Riverboat at Liberty Square

Fantasyland

Let your imagination sweep you away to a 'timeless land of enchantment' that makes everyone feel like a kid again. The breathtaking centerpiece of the newly expanded Fantasyland is Cinderella Castle which makes a perfect backdrop for your family photos. Stroll down memory lane with attractions based on Ariel, Dumbo, Winnie the Pooh, Peter Pan, Snow White, and Alice in Wonderland. A must-see for kids of all ages is the timeless attraction, it's a small world ®. You'll be humming this catchy tune for months to come! Be sure to visit the newest additions to Fantasyland, The Seven Dwarfs Mine Train and Under the Sea – Journey of the Little Mermaid.

The recently expanded Fantasyland features two main areas- Storybook Circus which opened in spring 2012, and Fantasyland Forest which opened in phases beginning in late 2012 and was completed in the spring of 2014. Storybook Circus features the return of The Barnstormer (formerly Goofy's Barnstormer) which was moved from the old Toontown, and the new Fantasyland train station. It is also home to Big Top Souvenirs and the Dumbo the Flying Elephant ride as well as several other minor attractions. Fantasyland Forest is inspired by Beauty and the Beast and The Little Mermaid and features two new castles as well as the previously mentioned Seven Dwarfs Mine Train and the Little Mermaid attraction. (More on those later.)

New Fantasyland at Magic Kingdom

Tomorrowland

You'll fcel like you've entered a science fiction story of a world that depicts the future that never was. You can rocket through space at Space Mountain, blast aliens at Buzz Lightyear's Space Ranger Spin, and zoom through the skies of Magic Kingdom on Astro Orbiter and the Tomorrowland Transit Authority. Enjoy silly jokes and slapstick comedy at the Monsters, Inc. Laugh Floor and keep Stitch out of trouble on Stitch's Great Escape.

Space Mountain and Buzz Lightyear are "can't miss" attractions, and don't forget to check out Walt Disney's animatronic adventure, Carousel of Progress which was originally created for the 1964 New York World's Fair.

Entrance to Tomorrowland

Magic Kingdom "Can't Miss" rides and attractions

While each ride and attraction is subject to your own personal tastes, here's a look at what I think are the "Can't Miss" attractions at Magic Kingdom.

"Wishes" Fireworks Show

Your trip to Magic Kingdom and Walt Disney World will not be complete until you've experienced the "Wishes" fireworks extravaganza! More than just a fireworks and projection show, "Wishes" takes you on a magical journey along with several Disney characters. It also includes a 'magical' appearance by Tinkerbell!

"Wishes" show at Cinderella Castle

Although you can see the show from just about anywhere in the park, you'll want to watch from the center of Main Street. The fireworks and lights are choreographed around

Cinderella Castle, and it just isn't the same without the castle front and center.

If you're traveling to Disney during peak seasons, be prepared to line up early, and stand elbow to elbow with other guests. Main Street and the surrounding areas will be packed. There's a good reason- it's worth it!

Although you'll certainly be exhausted after a long day at Walt Disney World's Magic Kingdom, you'll definitely want to stay for this show! If you don't want to get stuck in the big crowds during the mass exodus after the show, there are several shops along Main Street U.S.A. where you can wait it out. We love to stop at the Plaza Ice Cream Parlor after the fireworks. You should definitely try their 'create your own' ice cream sandwiches- they're delicious!!! You pick the cookies and the ice cream and the Plaza Ice Cream Parlor cast members do the rest.

Disney's Electrical Parade at Magic Kingdom

The show is preceded (and followed) by Disney's Electrical Parade down Main Street, U.S.A. The Electrical Parade features dozens of Disney floats and characters lit up with thousands of brilliantly colored flashing lights accompanied a beautiful musical score.

The parade begins near the barber shop at the beginning of Main Street; proceeds around the traffic circle in front of the main train station, and then onward down Main Street, U.S.A. toward Cinderella Castle. After moving around the traffic circle at the Castle, the parade continues on through Liberty Square before ending in Frontierland. This is another event you definitely won't want to miss!

Space Mountain

Prepare to blast-off to fun on Space Mountain

No trip to Magic Kingdom would be complete without blasting off on this perennial favorite. While certainly not up to the thrill level of some of today's super-coasters, Space Mountain is unique in that it is entirely indoors and completely dark throughout the ride- except for the star fields of course! Although this coaster barely tops 30 mph, the fact that it's in the dark makes it seem much faster. The excitement of not knowing whether you'll climb and dip, or twist and turn keeps you guessing and definitely adds to the thrill.

Big Thunder Mountain Railroad

Watch out as this rickety runaway train comes barreling down Thunder Mountain! You'll zoom through an abandoned mining town as the train pulls your mine car through a series of hills and turns. This ride is pretty bumpy so those with back or neck trouble may want to steer clear. Those brave enough to tackle Thunder Mountain will have as much fun enjoying the scenery as they will the ride itself!

The "Wildest ride in the Wilderness!"

Splash Mountain

Based on the obscure Disney tale, Song of the South, this ride is nonetheless pretty entertaining. You'll ride the rapids as you go into the mountain, seeing animatronic characters acting out various scenes from the tale. The music and animation are delightful. There are a few dips along the way that will tickle your tummy, but nothing too scary. Then...you get to the end.... and the big SPLASH! Fun, a little scary, and a great way to cool off!

Take the 'big plunge' at Splash Mountain

Buzz Lightyear's Space Ranger Spin

We ride this one a couple of times each time we visit Magic Kingdom. Nothing scary, it's just plain fun! You and a partner will blast aliens as you ride in a little space car around a track that winds through high-tech, futuristic scenes. The moving scenery has targets on it that you can blast for points with your laser. One person usually steers the car and shoots, while the other just shoots. It's fun to compete against others in your party to see who gets the highest score!

Take on Zurg in Space Ranger Spin

The Seven Dwarfs Mine Train

The Seven Dwarfs Mine Train was the last attraction added to the newly expanded Fantasyland. It opened during the spring of 2014, and has been jam packed ever since! Over the course of several Disney vacations, our family had the pleasure of seeing the ride progress from merely a pile of dirt a couple of years ago to the final product when we rode it several times during our visit shortly after the attraction opened in 2014. It was very cool to see the final product knowing (and seeing) just exactly how much work went into it.

Mine train construction in 2013

This family-oriented coaster is sort of a cross between the experience you'll enjoy on Big Thunder Mountain Railroad in Magic Kingdom's Frontierland and that of Goofy's Barnstormer located in the Storybook Circus section of Fantasyland. It's more of a thrill than Barnstormer, but not quite in the BTMR category, so it fits nicely in between the two as far as the ride experience.

Where Seven Dwarfs Mine Train differs from both, and from any other coaster in the world, is that the mine cars sway back and forth as you go around the track. Nothing drastic, but it's a nice touch as you swing out as you come around a bend and over dips and hill climbs.

Seven Dwarfs Mine Train is fun inside and out!

The scenery and soundtrack for the Mine Train is plucked directly from the Snow White and the Seven Dwarfs movie, and as usual Disney went all out to re-create a faithful rendition for this attraction. You'll make your way across rolling stone bridges and through the forest past the Dwarfs' cottage before plunging deep into the diamond mine where (of course) you'll find the dwarfs whistling while they work.

The Seven Dwarfs Mine Train is definitely a must-ride attraction at Magic Kingdom and is appropriate for the entire family. One word of caution though... This attraction is extremely popular so you'll want to ride it early (or late) in the day and you'll definitely want to schedule this one as one of your FastPass+ attractions if possible. Although the ride is tons of fun, it is also fairly short. If you spend two hours waiting in line for it, you may wish you hadn't.

Under the Sea – Voyage of the Little Mermaid

One of the new attractions in Magic Kingdom's New Fantasyland, Under the Sea – Voyage of the Little Mermaid is like taking a trip through animated scenes from the movie. Guests climb aboard their 'clamshell mobile' and enter Prince Eric's castle through an underground cavern as they plunge beneath the attraction's virtual waves to begin their journey.

The Audio-Animatronics and special-effects are outstanding

The Grand Finale

You'll enjoy the music of Sebastian the Crab, tap your toes or sing along to the movies most memorable tunes, and even have a chance to join a conga line as you embark on your journey. The Audio-Animatronics and scenery throughout the experience are some of Disney's best!

You'll see Ariel and Eric's first kiss, and splash into an ocean of the film's most beloved characters such as Sebastian, Flounder, and Scuttle. You'll even come face to face with Ursula, the Sea Witch as her 7+ foot tall and 12 foot wide character looms over you. You'll even get to celebrate Ariel and Eric's union as you take part in their fairytale wedding in the attraction's finale.

Be Our Guest restaurant

The grand two-story ballroom at Be Our Guest

Be Our Guest restaurant in the heart of the Beast's Castle in the Fantasyland Forest section of Magic Kingdom's Fantasyland is definitely a must-see attraction- that is IF you can get in. Dinner reservations at Be Our Guest are unquestionably one of the most sought-after reservations not only at Disney's Magic Kingdom theme park, but in all of Walt Disney World. The restaurant is booked solid for dinner six months in advance, and unless you get lucky, you will not have a very good chance to get in during the dinner hour. You have a much better chance of taking advantage of Be Our Guest's quick-service dining experience for lunch, but chances are you'll still be in for a long wait. Quick-service lunch menu options include Croque Monsier (grilled ham and cheese sandwich), Quinoa Salad, and a Carved Turkey Sandwich.

If you're lucky enough to land a table for dinner, you're in for a treat indeed! You'll be seated in one of three opulent dining rooms, and if you're seated in the mysterious West Wing you'll have the opportunity to view the enchanted rose as it loses its petals. The dinner menu consists of French and American cuisine with options such as Grilled Strip Steak, Coq au Vin Style Braised Pork, and Layered Ratatouille. The dessert options are a variety of beautifully decorated cupcakes that are simply out of this world!

Be sure to save room for dessert!

Be Our Guest is beautifully decorated and full of surprises. If you're lucky enough to have the opportunity to dine there, it will be an experience you won't soon forget!

Festival of Fantasy Parade

In the summer of 2014, Disney introduced a brand new daytime parade at Magic Kingdom- the Festival of Fantasy Parade. This afternoon parade begins in Frontierland and travels through Liberty Square before making the trek past Cinderella Castle and down Main Street U.S.A. where it concludes near the park entrance.

See familiar friends at Festival of Fantasy

This grand parade is Disney's biggest and best yet, and pays homage to the grand pageantry and characters of Disney's Fantasyland. You'll be treated to a plethora of Disney princesses such as Cinderella, Belle, and Elsa and Anna. See Peter and Wendy from Peter Pan soaring high through the sky aboard a pirate galleon as they try to escape the evil Captain Hook. You'll experience high-flying fun as Mickey and Minnie drift by in a giant hot-air balloon (see cover photo), and you'll see tons of other Disney favorites such as Pinocchio, Dumbo, and Snow White and the Seven Dwarfs too. The highlight and hottest part of the parade is the appearance of Maleficent when she appears as a fire-breathing dragon near the end of the parade.

The hottest parade in town!

If you're in the Magic Kingdom around 3:00 p.m., be sure to check out Disney's Festival of Fantasy Parade!

Disney's Magic Kingdom is certainly the crown-jewel of all the Disney parks. You're likely to spend a great deal of time exploring the magic during your Disney vacation. To find out even more about the park, including its history and a complete rundown of all the park's lands, attractions, and shows, be sure to check out Keys to the Kingdom: Your Complete Guide to Walt Disney World's Magic Kingdom Theme Park also available in paperback.

Epcot

The 2nd park to open at Walt Disney World was Disney's Epcot theme park. The Experimental Prototype Community of Tomorrow (EPCOT) was conceived by Walt Disney himself shortly before his death in 1966, and was one of the reasons he began to acquire land in the Orlando area during this time. Walt's vision of EPCOT was that it would "take its cue from the new ideas and new technologies that are emerging from the forefront of

American industry. It will be a community of tomorrow that will never be completed. It will always be showcasing and testing and demonstrating new materials and new systems."

You can still see the original architectural model for his planned city when you ride the Tomorrowland Transit Authority attraction at Magic Kingdom.

Entrance to Disney's Epcot theme park

Although it's mainly known for its international flavor thanks to its World Showcase, Disney's Epcot theme park has a variety of rides and attractions to entertain you for the entire day. Although Epcot lacks genuine thrill coasters, attractions such as Spaceship Earth, Test Track, and Mission: SPACE help make Epcot worth the trip. While in the park, you'll definitely want to check out Soarin', which was moved to Walt Disney World's Epcot theme park from Disneyland. Soarin' makes the trip worthwhile in and of itself!

Disney's Epcot theme park is composed of three sections: Future World East, Future World West, and World Showcase. The Future Worlds celebrate innovation and inventions on land, sea, sky, and space, and feature a number of hands-on and interactive exhibits. Future world is comprised of separate pavilions (see below), arranged in a circle around a central hub called Innoventions.

The other main section of Epcot is the World Showcase. The numerous pavilions of Epcot's World Showcase are arranged in a circle around the World Showcase Lagoon. You can walk completely around the lagoon (a very long walk!) to visit each country, or you can take a ferry across the lagoon to either of two points on the other side.

Future World Pavilions

Here's a brief overview of the nine pavilions that make up Epcot's Future World.

Spaceship Earth

When you enter Epcot through the main entrance, you'll walk right under Spaceship Earth. It is the large geodesic dome that is the symbol of Disney's Epcot theme park. Spaceship Earth features a ride inside to the top of the dome, and an interactive play area with lots of entertaining activities for kids and grownups too!

Innoventions East & Innoventions West

These matching areas are the first two pavilions you'll encounter after passing Spaceship Earth. These pavilions both feature a glimpse into the future, highlighting emerging technologies like robots in a way that's interesting to kids. Both pavilions feature interactive games, exhibits, simulations, and activities designed to entertain and inform kids of all ages.

Inside the dome: Spaceship Earth

At Innoventions East you'll find activities focusing on the different ways our world continues to change. You'll learn about green living, health and wellness, and the effects of extreme weather. There's even a chance to design and ride your own thrill ride in The Sum of All Thrills roller coaster simulator.

The Innoventions West pavilion features exhibits focusing on computer technology, finance, and fire safety. Youngsters will get a chance to embark on The Great Piggy

Bank Adventure to learn the importance of saving for life goals, and they can also check out some of the latest technologies at the Videogame Playground.

Innoventions Pavilion

Learn about fire safety at Where's the Fire?

Universe of Energy

The Universe of Energy Pavilion helps kids learn about energy and natural resources. The tour is co-hosted by

Ellen DeGeneres and Bill Nye the Science Guy. Take a journey through space and time in Ellen's Energy Adventure, a 45-minute multimedia romp that takes you back to the beginning of our universe with a Big Bang. You'll travel through dinosaur-laden forests and escape streams of molten lava as you explore the effects of energy from past to present.

Mission: SPACE

If you've always wondered what it would be like to pilot a spaceship on a journey to Mars, but just never quite got around to signing up for astronaut training, then Mission: Space may be your perfect ticket to an adventure of a lifetime. This space simulator features both a regular and a 'light' version. The original (regular) version simulates the extreme G-forces felt during a space launch. The 'light' version is the same attraction minus the centrifuge that is used to create the G-forces felt in the regular version.

Mission: SPACE entrance

Once aboard your spacecraft, you and the other three space cadets in your crew will assume important roles for the duration of your journey. Choose between navigator, pilot, commander, or flight engineer, and strap in to prepare for liftoff. During the mission, you'll be asked to execute a series of tasks (which vary by role) in order to ensure a safe and successful trip to the red planet.

The mission is counting on you- don't let us down!

Test Track

This recently re-imagined attraction will take you through a gamut of road tests- all in a car that you design! Once you make your way to the front of the queue, you'll visit the Chevrolet Design Center to design your very own car or truck. Then, you'll get to put your "SIM Car" through the paces on the fastest ride in all of Walt Disney World! (Read more about Test Track in the Epcot "Can't Miss Attractions" section later in this chapter.)

Designing your car is half the fun!

Imagination

The Imagination Pavilion is a short diversion from the excitement of some of the other pavilions, but will still keep you entertained for an hour or so. The return of the 3-D film, the "Captain EO" attraction is here, as is the ImageWorks area. At ImageWorks, kids can pose for a digital picture and use image editing tools to add all sorts of cool (and crazy) special effects.

The Land

The Land Pavilion features the highlight of all highlights at Epcot (and all of Walt Disney World for that matter) Soarin'. This hang gliding simulation will have you truly amazed as you absorb the sights, sounds, and scents of the California scenery. You'll also find Living with the Land and The Circle of Life attractions here- both of which are worthy of a visit.

The Seas

Learn about our friends living underwater in The Seas pavilion. The highlight of The Seas is Turtle Talk with Crush, an amazing interactive feature that encourages audience participation. You can talk to the animated turtle, Crush, and he responds to you! The Seas pavilion also features beautiful saltwater aquarium that holds nearly 6 million gallons of water, and a fun attraction called The Seas with Nemo & Friends in which you climb aboard a 'clamshell mobile' to embark on a journey through Nemo's world.

Epcot World Showcase

The World Showcase pavilions are what truly give Epcot its international flavor. The World Showcase features pavilions dedicated to 11 different countries. All of the pavilions feature shops, restaurants, and architecture of the host nation, and all are staffed by citizens of the countries they represent. A handful of these pavilions also house a ride or show to enhance the international experience.

Turtle Talk with Crush is fun AND educational!

The 11 nations of the Epcot World Showcase (arranged in a circle around the World Showcase Lagoon) are: Mexico, Norway, China, Germany, Italy, America, Japan, Morocco, France, the United Kingdom, and Canada.

The countries below offer a ride or attraction in addition to the shops, food, and architecture.

Canada

The Canada Pavilion features a Circle-Vision film starring Martin Short called "O Canada!" Parents beware- no strollers are allowed in this feature, and everyone stands during the show (for the best views). For this reason, families with small children may choose to pass on this one.

United Kingdom pavilion at Epcot

France

Like most of the international pavilions with an attraction, the France Pavilion features a short film. Rather than the 360 degree view films shown in the Canada and China pavilions, Impressions de France is shown on a 200-degree wide-screen. You'll enjoy this 20 minute feature, and there's no waiting as shows run on the ½ hour.

United States

The American Adventure is the feature attraction at the United States Pavilion. This multimedia presentation features animatronic figures combined with video to deliver an entertaining look at American history. See Benjamin Franklin, Thomas Jefferson, and many other prominent figures from U.S. history plucked right out of the history books and into this patriotic 30-minute presentation.

Ben Franklin in 'The American Adventure'

China

The China Pavilion features Reflections of China, an inside look at a country which is still a mystery to many. Although the film features nice views of the Great Wall of China, and panoramic views of the scenery of the Country, it looks a little dated and is missing one of the coolest symbols of China- the Giant Panda.

Norway

For years, the Norway Pavilion has featured an entertaining boat ride called Maelstrom. Visitors would get a chance to climb aboard a 16 passenger Viking Ship to tour the fjords, waterfalls, and other scenery in this beautiful country. In September of 2014, Disney announced that Maelstrom would close to make way for a brand new Frozen-themed attraction in the Norway pavilion. The new attraction is sure to be a big hit when it opens in 2016.

Mexico

Epcot's Mexico Pavilion

The Mexico Pavilion features a nice little boat ride that showcases the scenery and culture of the country. Join the animated Three Caballeros (including Donald Duck) on this short entertaining journey.

Epcot "Can't Miss" rides and attractions

Here's a look at the things you want to make sure you see and do during your visit to Epcot:

IllumiNations

With its laser lights, fireworks, synchronized fountains, and rousing music, the IllumiNations closing show at Epcot is thought by many to be the best of all closing shows at Walt Disney World. IllumiNations takes place over the World Showcase lagoon and you can expect MAJOR crowds. Although the crowds are very large for this show, you should be able to find a decent viewing area right up until show time due to the sheer vastness of the World Showcase Lagoon in which it takes place. Like the Wishes closing show at Magic Kingdom, there's a reason for the big crowds- it's worth it!

You won't want to miss IllumiNations!

The show centers on a large globe in the lagoon and can be seen from anywhere in the area. If you watch IllumiNations from near the Mexico pavilion, or at the south side of the lagoon, you'll be able to beat many of the crowds as they head toward the main park exit at the close of the show.

Add IllumiNations to your list of must-do activities on your next Disney vacation!

The giant globe that is the centerpiece of Illuminations

Test Track

The recently re-imagined Test Track sponsored by Chevrolet expands on the original concept for the attraction and dials it up to new levels for even more thrills and excitement. After you reach the front of the queue (which could take a while- this attraction consistently has one of the longest wait times in all of Walt Disney World) you'll enter the Chevrolet Design Center to have the opportunity to design your test vehicle. That's right- each rider gets a chance to design their own car!

Inside the Chevrolet Design Center

After scanning your Magic Band or park ticket to login, you'll advance through a series of menus where you'll have a chance to choose the type, size, and color of your vehicle, and have a myriad of other options to choose from as you outfit your virtual machine. Vehicles are rated on a scale of 1-100 based on the following criteria: capability (handling), efficiency (fuel-efficiency and environmental friendliness), power (speed), and responsiveness (maneuverability). Each time you change a parameter, you'll see the effect it has on your vehicle in real-time. This gives you the ability to tweak your options as you progress through the design process. After you've completed your design, it's off to the track!

Don't forget to pick up your ride photo!

Test Track replicates road tests performed at the GM proving grounds to give riders a true sense of what goes into the design and testing of new vehicles. The scenery is completely redesigned, but the overall ride experience is similar to that of the original.

Passengers are loaded into simulated test vehicles, up to six in a car that travel individually around the track. Riders take their vehicles through a gamut of tests including acceleration and braking, sharp turns, bumpy roads, and how the car responds to heat and cold. After each test, your SIM Car will slow down to give you the opportunity to see how the vehicle you designed fared on the test. The ride culminates with an exhilarating lap around the test track including high-banked turns, at 65 miles per hour! Although the coolest part of the ride (the lap around the test track) is at the end and over very quickly, Test Track is a unique experience from start to finish and a pretty exciting one too!

Flying along at 64.7 MPH on Test Track!

Although the ride ends when you disembark your vehicle, the experience doesn't end there. On the way out, you'll want to stop by the big board to see how your vehicle rates against all the other vehicles hitting the test track that day. There's also a neat simulator where you can race your car again on a virtual course, and don't forget to check out some of the great Chevy cars displayed in the mini showroom at the exit.

Test Track is frequently the longest (and slowest moving) line of all the attractions at Epcot. Although the Chevrolet Design Center is a cool feature, and certainly adds a great deal to the attraction, it also adds time to your wait in line. This attraction is one that is definitely worthy of using as one of your FastPass+ reservations. That will get you through the queues faster, and will free up more of your day to explore the other fun things to do at Epcot.

Soarin'

Soarin' at Disney's Epcot theme park is one attraction you certainly won't want to miss! Have you ever wondered what it would be like to hang-glide up in the clouds, then swoop down over the Golden Gate bridge? Fly low over an orange grove then ski down the mountains of California? If the thought of experiencing those things (and more!) intrigues you, then be sure to ride Soarin!

The ride begins with riders strapping in to one of three banks of seats with their feet dangling below them. At the front of the theater is a giant movie screen. When you're cleared for takeoff, the lights go down and you're lifted high into the air. When the show begins, you're up in the clouds, soon to swoop down over San Francisco Bay! The chairs of this hang gliding simulator sway gently as you ride the thermals over various pieces of California scenery. (The ride was moved to Walt Disney World from Disneyland in California.)

Climb aboard Soarin'

Adding to the realism is the fact that you'll smell the orange groves and the ocean breeze, and you'll feel the mist as you dip down over the ocean. Soarin' is truly a unique attraction and one you need to experience to truly appreciate! There are even interactive games you can play while waiting in line. Competing against the other groups of riders in various fun activities sure makes the wait in line go faster!

Swoop down over the Golden Gate Bridge in Soarin'

Spaceship Earth

Although Spaceship Earth is certainly no 'thrill ride', it's an enjoyable experience and will be a nice break from all the walking you'll do while at Epcot. Plus, it's great for those people who have always wondered what's in 'the big ball' (or 'geodesic dome' if you want to get technical) that has become the symbol of Epcot.

You board your spaceship to begin your journey through time. As you slowly traverse upward, you enter some basic information about yourself and pose for a picture. History will unfold before you as you progress to the top of the dome. Near the end of your experience you'll answer a number of questions about the vision you have for your future. At the end of the ride you'll catch a glimpse of your future- complete with your face in the pictures. You can even have a postcard emailed to you from your own future!

After you exit the ride there are many interactive exhibits to enjoy, and you get to see yourself projected on a large globe along with the faces of other recent visitors. It's fun to see the many different countries represented. All and all, Spaceship Earth is a pretty enjoyable experience.

See the past and future in Spaceship Earth

Hollywood Studios

As the name implies, Disney's Hollywood Studios is a tribute to the glitz, glamour, and history of Hollywood, and the film and television industries. Hollywood Studios features a variety of thrill rides and live entertainment that will entertain both kids and adults.

The good news is that Hollywood Studios is the smallest of the parks at Disney World. This will make things a bit easier on your aching feet. The bad news is that its layout is not as intuitive and easy to navigate as the other theme parks. Rather than utilizing the spoke and hub design of parks such as Magic Kingdom and Epcot, Disney's Hollywood Studios uses a series of "Boulevards" to connect the different areas of the park.

Hollywood Studios entrance

While the abundance of street signs will certainly prevent you from getting lost in the park, you'll want to make sure you have a map handy to help you get around the park in the most efficient manner.

Disney's Hollywood Studios is a park slated to undergo many changes, some rumored and others confirmed over the next several years. A long-standing favorite at

Hollywood Studios since 2009, The American Idol Experience was closed at the end of August, 2014. The location was temporarily used to house the "For the First Time in Forever – a 'Frozen' Sing-Along Celebration late in 2014, but as of this writing an official replacement for the attraction has yet to be announced.

The American Idol Experience had a good run

The end of 2014 also saw the end of the Studio Backlot Tour, an opening-day attraction at Hollywood Studios. After a run of more than 25 years as part of the Streets of America section of the park, the Studio Backlot Tour came to an end on Saturday, September 27th, 2014. One rumor for the re-use of the vast amount of land occupied by the attraction is for Disney to create a duplicate of the hugely popular Radiator Springs Racers, part of Cars Land at Disney's California Adventure theme park, although nothing is confirmed at this time.

Other rumors surrounding changes coming to Disney's Hollywood Studios include the ending of the Indiana Jones Epic Stunt Spectacular! show in the Echo Lake section of the park, and the possible closing or re-imagining of the famed Lights, Motors, Action! Extreme Stunt Show, a staple in the Streets of America section of Hollywood Studios since 2005. Both sets of rumors have the attractions becoming part of a new a Star Wars and/or

Cars Land sections of the park respectively. At this time, the Indiana Jones speculation seems to be more credible, but we'll just have to wait and see. It's clear that whatever happens, Hollywood Studios is on the verge of some major changes. Stay tuned.

My big stunt show debut- Could this be the end for Indy?

One final change to Hollywood Studios, a big one confirmed by Disney, is the removal of the giant Sorcerer Mickey hat icon that was added to the park during the 100 Years of Magic celebration in 2001. While this icon has been considered as an eyesore by many WDW purists who preferred the original look of the park, it has been an integral part of Hollywood Studios for me, and I'm going to miss it. The one constant with Disney parks is change, so I guess it's time to move forward.

Below are the main areas of Disney's Hollywood Studios theme park.

Hollywood Boulevard

Hollywood Boulevard at Disney's Hollywood Studios is the equivalent of Main Street at Disney's Magic Kingdom. Stores and shops line the street located at the entrance to the park, and you'll occasionally find actors performing short skits to entertain the crowd. The Hollywood Studios parade runs along this route which is also home to The Great Movie Ride. Although The Great Movie Ride is the only attraction at Hollywood Studios located on Hollywood Boulevard, the boulevard is also home to the famous Hollywood Brown Derby restaurant, and a number of unique shops such as Mickey's of Hollywood, Keystone Clothiers, and Adrian & Edith's Head to Toe- a shop specializing in embroidery where you can get your hats, apparel, and towels personalized to make your Disney memories even more special.

Hollywood Boulevard

Echo Lake

Although Echo Lake lacks a particular theme, it IS home to a couple of Hollywood Studios prime attractions: Indiana Jones Epic Stunt Spectacular and Star Tours. Indiana Jones is an exciting stunt show re-enacting scenes from the movie series. Star Tours is a Star Wars motion simulator that lets you enter the Star Wars universe by re-enacting scenes from George Lucas' epic franchise. The Tatooine Traders Star Wars gift shop located at the Star Tours exit is a great place to pick up a variety of Star Wars souvenirs.

Echo Lake is also home to several restaurants such as Hollywood & Vine and the 50's Prime Time Café. You'll also find quick-service dining options such as Min and Bill's Dockside Diner, Backlot Express, and the Oasis Canteen for snacks.

Relive the excitement of Indiana Jones

Streets of America

Streets of America provides examples of the work that goes into making Hollywood movie sets. Backdrop paintings and street scenes are used to re-create places like New York City and San Francisco. Streets of America is also home to Hollywood Studios attractions such as the Muppet Vision 3-D movie and the highly entertaining Lights, Motors, Action! Extreme Stunt Show.

If you're looking for a place to eat while visiting Streets of America, stop in at Mama Melrose's Ristorante Italiano for brick-oven pizza, pasta, chicken and the like, or check out the Pizza Planet Arcade for great pizza and video game action.

San Francisco in Streets of America

Mickey Avenue

Mickey Avenue lacks the style of some of the other streets at Disney's Hollywood Studios, and with the closing of the Studio Backlot tour which provided insight into how action scenes from blockbuster films are created, it is home only to the Walt Disney: One Man's Dream attraction. One Man's Dream is an interesting multimedia gallery detailing the history of animation and other interesting historical elements depicting Walt Disney's rise to fame. It also includes a bit of history about Walt Disney World. Mickey Avenue also houses a mini-theater that shows a 15-minute film that brings the story of Walt Disney to life.

Animation Courtyard

Sandwiched between Mickey Avenue and Echo Lake is Disney's Animation Courtyard. Animation Courtyard at Disney's Hollywood Studios is home to attractions such as Voyage of the Little Mermaid, a live show in a unique indoor theater, the Disney Junior stage show, and the Animation Gallery gift shop. It is also home to The Magic of Disney Animation attraction where you can sit with a real Disney artist and learn a bit about the animation process and how it's used to create cartoons. You'll also get to draw one of your favorite Disney characters which is great fun for all ages. You'll even get to take your drawing home with you- it makes a great (free!) souvenir and keepsake to help capture the memories of your Walt Disney World vacation.

Pixar Place

Pixar Place is home to Toy Story Midway Mania!

Pixar Place is the newest area of Hollywood Studios and it has Toy Story Midway Mania to thank for its spot on the Hollywood Studios map. Toy Story is the only attraction at Pixar Place and it also happens to be the most popular attraction (with the longest lines) in all of Walt Disney World. Pixar place is also home to a character meet and greet with Toy Story favorites Buzz Lightyear & Woody.

Sunset Boulevard

To the right of Hollywood Boulevard at Disney's Hollywood Studios, you'll find one of the most exciting areas of the park- Sunset Boulevard. Sunset Boulevard is home to the two most exciting thrill-rides at Hollywood Studios, and perhaps all of Walt Disney World. Rock 'n' Roller Coaster is an exciting indoor coaster featuring the ageless rock band Aerosmith. Don't miss the Twilight Zone Tower of Terror, a haunting ride featuring a series of random sudden drops. Sunset Boulevard is also home to the Beauty and the Beast stage show, and the outdoor amphitheater that is home to Hollywood Studios' awesome Fantasmic! closing show.

Beauty and the Beast stage show

Hollywood Studios "Can't Miss" rides and attractions

Disney's Hollywood Studios has some of the coolest rides in all of Walt Disney World, and arguably the best closing show. Whether you're looking for thrill rides, shows, or just something a little different, Hollywood Studios has something for you! Here's a look at some top picks for rides and attractions at Disney's Hollywood Studios theme park.

Fantasmic!

The Fantasmic! closing show at Disney's Hollywood Studios is unique in that it is part pyrotechnics, part stage show, part parade, and TOTAL entertainment! The show takes place nightly in front of nearly 7,000 guests at the Hollywood Studios outdoor amphitheater.

While the production will never earn an award for its plot, it does feature Mickey in the role as the Sorcerer's Apprentice battling off hordes of evil Disney characters. While it's a little scary at times for the younger kids, it should be fine for most. One cool effect is when film images are projected onto a screen of cascading water- very unique indeed!

The shows are usually held twice each evening, but only once during less crowded times of the year. Times also vary depending on the time of year. You'll want to get there as much as 45 minutes to an hour early to make sure you get a seat. Best viewing is center stage about half way up, but truthfully there isn't a bad seat in the house. The later show is usually less crowded, so if you're attending that show you may not need to get there quite as early.

One way to guarantee your seat at this always packed show is to book the Fantasmic! Dinner Package. You'll choose whether to dine at the Hollywood Brown Derby, Mama Melrose's Ristorante Italiano, or the ever popular

Hollywood & Vine restaurant, and then be guaranteed priority seating for that night's extravaganza. A great way to enjoy a delicious dinner and a great show!

Sorcerer Mickey in Fantasmic!

Rock 'n' Roller Coaster

Rock 'n' Roller Coaster featuring Aerosmith is possibly the best pure 'thrill-coaster' in all of Walt Disney World. You begin the ride in the studio with the band, catching the end of a recording session. They need to cut it short in order to make it to the show on time, and they invite you to come along. You move to the next room while you wait for your limo to arrive. That's right- the roller coaster looks like a super stretch limousine!

After traffic clears, you burn rubber- going from zero to the top speed of nearly 60 mph in a matter of seconds. The ride is entirely indoors, and parts of the ride are in the dark- lit only by the street signs. With blaring music (by Aerosmith of course) pumping out of the limo's sound system, you'll rock to the music as you twist and turn down the freeway going through three inversions before screeching to a stop- arriving just in time for the start of the show. A true thrill from start to finish made that much better by the rock and roll premise behind the experience. FastPass+ is a must for this attraction as it frequently has wait times approaching (and sometimes exceeding) two hours.

3...2....1.... GO!!!!

Twilight Zone Tower of Terror

Tucked into the trees at the end of Sunset Boulevard and looming ominously in the distance as you approach, is the infamous Hollywood Tower Hotel- sight of the Twilight Zone Tower of Terror. This exhilarating experience has been one of the premier attractions at Disney's Hollywood Studios since its debut in July of 1994. This attraction is definitely worthy of one of your FastPass+ reservations as it frequently has extended wait times throughout the day. Certainly not in the league of Toy Story Midway Mania, or even Rock 'n' Roller Coaster, but long waits nonetheless.

As soon as you enter the hotel lobby, you'll be immersed in a haunting experience. You'll enter a room that immediately goes dark after a loud thunderclap as you watch a video hosted by Rod Serling, the creator of the old Twilight Zone television series, which sets the stage for the attraction. (Yes- it is really Rod Serling in the video.

Although he died nearly 20 years before Disney began work on the attraction, Disney used a little 'magic' and a celebrity impersonator to voiceover parts of the dialogue to bring you the introduction.)

Tower of Terror

You'll be seated aboard a rickety old freight (or should I say 'fright'?) elevator that will soon begin moving through the haunted hallways of the hotel, stopping several times along the way to present the spooky scenes leading up to the climax of the ride.

Once you enter the tower, you'll zip to the top and be dropped suddenly (and randomly) down several floors at a time. The ride is controlled by a series of varied pre-programmed sequences meaning you can ride it over and over, and have a different experience each time. You'll never know what to expect other than the fact that the ride will be a terrifying, memorable, and unique experience each time you ride.

The halls of the hotel are filled with frights

Lights, Motors, Action! – Extreme Stunt Show

Anyone with a passing interest in high-speed car chases, shootouts, and motorcycle stunts should go see the Lights, Motors, Action! – Extreme Stunt Show at Disney's Hollywood Studios. Although rumors of this attraction's demise are rampant, at the time of this writing, the show is still alive and well. For as long as the show continues, if you attend you'll see a variety of action sequences 'live' and then watch them played back in slow motion on a large video screen as the stunt coordinator explains how they're filmed. It's a truly unique experience to see how the cameras are setup for filming the various stunts, and to get an inside look at the special cars and equipment involved in bringing the stunts to life. If you're lucky, you'll get to see the motorcycle stunt-guy start on fire during one of the action sequences. There is even a special appearance by Lightning McQueen from the Cars movie franchise!

Things get pretty hot at Lights, Motors, Action!

Toy Story Midway Mania

A trip to Disney's Hollywood Studios would hardly be complete without at least one ride on the most popular attraction in all of Walt Disney World, Toy Story Midway Mania. The attraction has been hugely popular since it opened at Hollywood Studios in May of 2008, and its appeal has remained strong throughout the maturation of the Disney-Pixar Toy Story franchise.

The fun begins in the queue with Mr. Potato Head

The ride takes place in Andy's room where his toys have assembled a variety of carnival games as part of Andy's birthday celebration. This rootin', tootin' shootin' match (as Disney calls it) consists of a series of shooting games such as Hamm & Eggs where you'll get a chance to blast a series of both stationary and moving barnyard animal targets by launching hardboiled eggs at them, and Buzz Lightyear's Flying Tossers where you'll flip a series of rings at various space-based targets such as a variety of aliens and rocket ships. My personal favorite is the Green Army Men Shoot Camp where you get a chance to toss baseballs to break plates at the green army men firing range. The sights and sounds are such that you feel as if you're actually breaking real plates- not merely seeing a 3-D video image of the plates breaking.

There are five games in all, and after each you'll see your score (including number of hits and accuracy) before being whooshed off, twisting and turning to the next level. At the end of the ride, you'll find out if you were the highest score in your car. (There are four people in each car, one next to you and two behind you that you can't see.)

Expect non-stop action at Toy Story Midway Mania

You're sure to be exhausted by the end of the ride- or at least have two very sore arms from pulling the cord to fire during each level. All in all, Toy Story Midway Mania is a great experience for kids of all ages.

Animal Kingdom

Take your favorite zoo and 'turbo charge' it. Then add some thrill rides, stage shows, and authentic scenery. What do you have? Why it's Walt Disney World's Animal Kingdom of course! You'll have a wild time at Disney's Animal Kingdom theme park whether you're roaming amongst the wild animals in Kilimanjaro Safaris, searching for the Yeti on Expedition Everest, or just learning about wildlife conservation at Rafiki's Planet Watch.

One advantage Animal Kingdom has over the other parks in Walt Disney World is an abundance of shade! The lush surroundings provide relief from the hot Florida sun, and there seems to be less walking than in the other parks. When it all gets to be too much, cool off with a wild ride down the Kali River Rapids!

The entrance to Animal Kingdom

Lands of Animal Kingdom

Walt Disney World's Animal Kingdom is based on the same 'hub and spoke' layout utilized by Disney's Magic Kingdom and Epcot theme parks. It is made up of five lands that make up the 'spokes'. They are arranged around Discovery Island which is the center hub of Disney's Animal Kingdom. A sixth land, Camp Minnie-Mickey, was closed in early 2014 to make way for a new Avatar-themed area expected to open at Animal Kingdom in early 2017. Here's a brief overview of each of the lands of Disney's Animal Kingdom:

Oasis

Although the Oasis is really nothing more than the entrance to Disney's Animal Kingdom, and provides no attractions, it becomes a vital part of the Animal Kingdom experience as you traverse the winding paths into the jungle. Oasis is also home to the Rainforest Café which has entrances both inside and outside of the park. It also features guest services, lockers, and an ATM.

Discovery Island

Once you pass through the Oasis area of Animal Kingdom after entering the park, you'll cross the bridge to the tranquil paths and exotic trails of Discovery Island. Discovery Island is the center hub of Disney's Animal Kingdom and is the main thoroughfare that leads to the other areas of the park. As you stroll down the paths traversing Discovery Island you'll encounter a variety of wildlife along the way as the island is home to white stork, red kangaroo, the Galapagos tortoise and many other species.

Intricate carvings in The Tree of Life

The Tree of Life soars high above the island and features over 300 animal carvings celebrating the diversity and harmony of nature. Among the carvings are lions, deer, eagles, monkeys, scorpions and dolphins. It's fun to stop and see how many different animals you can find.

Inside the Tree of Life is Discovery Island's only attraction, It's Tough to be a Bug! It's Tough to be a Bug! is a 3D film and live action Audio-Animatronics show inspired by the Disney-Pixar film, A Bug's Life. If a journey through the land of creepy crawlies sounds like fun, then don your 3D glasses and take a journey into a bug's life at It's Tough to be a Bug!

Africa

Kilimanjaro Safaris is the highlight of Africa at Disney's Animal Kingdom. You'll tour the African plains in an open air SUV as you wind through the habitats of lions, elephants, giraffes, rhinos, hippos, and more. Also take a stroll through the Pangani Forest Exploration Trail to see a variety of other African wildlife.

Kilimanjaro Safaris

Africa is also home to the Festival of the Lion King show, recently transplanted from the now defunct Camp Minnie-Mickey, and is the boarding point for the Wildlife Express Train that takes you to Rafiki's Planet Watch.

Should the growling you hear be in your stomach, and not coming from one of the animal exhibits, there are a variety of dining options in Africa as well. Visit the Tusker House Restaurant for a casual family buffet of traditional African cuisine, or grab a coffee and sandwich at the Kusafiri Coffee Shop & Bakery.

Rafiki's Planet Watch

You can only visit Rafiki's Planet Watch by riding the Wildlife Express Train that boards near the Pangani Forest Exploration Trail. This exhibit gives guests a behind the scenes look into what it takes to run Disney's Animal Kingdom, and provides an insightful overview into conservation, animal care, and endangered species. You can visit the Affection Section petting yard, and kids can meet Rafiki himself as well as Jiminy Cricket.

Asia

The highlights of Asia are Kali River Rapids and Expedition Everest. Kali River Rapids is an exhilarating white water rafting ride through a man-made canyon, and Expedition Everest is an exciting rollercoaster that features a wild train ride up the world's tallest mountain in an authentically icy setting. While in Asia, you can also visit the Maharajah Jungle Trek to see Bengal tigers, Komodo dragons, and lots of bats too!

Asia is also home to the Flights of Wonder show featuring exotic birds. If food or drink is what you need, Asia offers Bradley Falls and Mr. Kamal's as quick-service options.

You can also grab a beer or margarita at Upcountry, or enjoy a complete meal featuring Pan-Asian cuisine at the Yak & Yeti restaurant.

Beware of the Yeti in Expedition Everest

Dinoland U.S.A.

In DinoLand U.S.A. at Disney's Animal Kingdom, you'll get a chance to go back in time in Dinosaur- an exciting thrill ride where you'll encounter a T-Rex! The Primeval Whirl, a carnival-style roller coaster with lots of twists and turns is here, as is the Boneyard where kids can play in the dinosaur-themed play area. Finding Nemo- the Musical is also in DinoLand U.S.A. It's a delightful stage & special effects show based on the movie.

Animal Kingdom "Can't Miss" rides and attractions

Disney's Animal Kingdom offers a refreshing change of pace from the other parks. Although there are plenty of rides and attractions, the stars of the shows are the animals themselves. While everyone who visits Animal Kingdom should be sure to check out the wildlife in Kilimanjaro Safaris, here are some other 'Can't Miss' attractions at Walt Disney World's Animal Kingdom.

Expedition Everest

Search for the Yeti on Expedition Everest

It's "All aboard!" as you climb this mountain train for a trip up Mount Everest in this exciting roller coaster. Located in

Asia, this coaster is the most popular ride at Animal Kingdom, and one of the most exciting in all of Walt Disney World. You'll want to get to this one early- or schedule it as one of your FastPass+ attractions to make the most of the ride, and your day at Animal Kingdom.

You'll go forward **and** backward on this wild thrill ride amongst glaciers, icy cliffs, and bamboo forests. You'll even come face to face with the Yeti as he roams the icy mountains!

Although this coaster is exciting enough to give teens and grown-ups a thrilling ride, it's not too scary for the little ones. So, if they're tall enough, have them give it a go!

Kali River Rapids

Ride the rapids in this family-style water ride that is sure to leave the whole family soaked! The Kali River winds through the jungles of Asia taking each eight-passenger raft through rapids, waterfalls, and even geysers! The raft slowly turns as you travel down the river, so depending on where you're sitting you may get completely soaked- or just really, really wet!

Cool off in Kali River Rapids

There's even a bridge with water cannons where previous riders or passersby can wait- ready to douse you with water! Be sure to put cameras or other electronics in the storage bin at the center of the raft- you certainly don't want them to get as soaked as you!

Although the ride has its thrilling moments (as you wait to see who gets the wettest) it's not too scary for little kids. If they're tall enough to take along (38 inches or taller) they'll have a blast!

Kilimanjaro Safaris

Animals are up close and personal on Kilimanjaro Safaris

A trip to Animal Kingdom would not be complete without a trek on Kilimanjaro Safaris! You and your traveling companions will climb aboard a very large safari vehicle for a trip through Africa! This ride is NOT like any zoo exhibit you'll ever see- you'll be riding amongst the animals! You'll see lions, elephants, giraffes, hippos, exotic birds, and many more species in close replications of their natural habitats. Occasionally, the driver will need to stop the vehicle to let a giraffe, rhinoceros, or other animal cross the road- just watch out for poachers! This is a very cool experience you have to see to believe!

Festival of the Lion King

When you've had enough of the African heat and blizzards of Everest, and after you've cooled off in Kali River Rapids, head over to Africa for a change of pace to check out one of Animal Kingdom's awesome shows. Festival of the Lion King is a very entertaining Broadway-style show, performed 'in the round' in an air conditioned theater.

Check out Festival of the Lion King at Camp Minnie-Mickey

The show encourages audience participation, and faithfully re-creates the Lion King movie. Simba, Rafiki, Timon, Pumba, and their friends are joined by a host of jungle performers to keep you entertained throughout this ½ hour show. We really enjoyed watching the monkey acrobats pull off amazing maneuvers on the trapeze and trampolines, and the fire dancers were pretty cool too! For a great way to beat the heat and be entertained at the same time, check out Festival of the Lion King at Disney's Animal Kingdom!

Finding Nemo – The Musical

Just across the bridge from Expedition Everest on the outskirts of DinoLand U.S.A. sits one of the most amazing and unique puppet shows you'll ever see- it's Finding Nemo – The Musical. This 40-minute stage show features a myriad of special effects and 14 original songs that tell the story of Nemo and his deep sea adventures.

Be sure to check out Finding Nemo – The Musical

You'll plunge into the deepest, darkest depths of the ocean as the theater magically transforms into an underwater paradise. As the story progresses, you'll visit with familiar friends such as Marlin, Dory, and Crush as you follow their adventures along the Great Barrier Reef. Actors in unique costumes tell the story with the aid of giant hand-held puppets that make this nautical adventure one of the must "sea" attractions at Animal Kingdom.

6) Walt Disney World Water Parks

If you're looking to venture beyond the four great theme parks of Walt Disney World, you should definitely check out Disney's awesome water parks: Typhoon Lagoon and Blizzard Beach. If you get the Water Park Fun & More option on your Disney tickets, you'll get a visit to one of these 'extra' attractions for each day of your park pass. For example, a six day park pass with this option will give you six visits to the water parks. If you don't need quite that many water park visits during your stay, you can instead use your extra passes at a variety of other Disney attractions (or the '& More' portion of the ticket). See chapter 3 Disney Ticket Information for more details.

Cool off at Typhoon Lagoon & Blizzard Beach!

Both of Disney's water parks host over 2 million visitors a year making them the most visited water parks in the world. Both also offer a variety of water slides, a wave pool, and several other attractions that will give you plenty to do for an entire day- or even for a couple of days if you're spending a week (or more) at Walt Disney World. Both offer activities for adults, teens, tweens, and younger kids too.

When you visit the water parks, it's a good idea to bring your own towel- though they're available for rental at each park. You're also welcome to bring in coolers to both parks- no glass or alcohol please. Wear a comfortable pair of water shoes if you have them. Your feet will thank you after hours of walking around on the hot pavement. You may want to plan to rent a locker to store your valuables, or better yet leave them locked in your room or your car. I always bring a waterproof pouch to store my car keys, some spending cash, and our park tickets (during trips we stay off-property). They're available in a variety of sizes which comes in handy if you need room for a cell phone or small camera too, and you can buy ones that go around your neck, or strap to your waist. If you're staying at a Disney resort, or have purchased a magic band, make sure you stow it away while you're in the wave pools or going down the slides. On our last trip, my son's magic band was lost at the foot of Mount Mayday in the Typhoon Lagoon Surf Pool. While this was not a huge deal (we had an extra one that we could re-activate) it will still be an inconvenience you do not need to risk.

Read on, to learn more about Typhoon Lagoon & Blizzard Beach!

Typhoon Lagoon

The premise behind Disney's 56-acre Typhoon Lagoon water park is that a huge storm has swept through a tropical island leaving the park in ruins in its wake. The surging waters have left behind numerous water slides, and have marooned the Ms. Tilly fishing trawler atop Mount Mayday. Since its opening in June of 1989, the highlight and centerpiece of Typhoon Lagoon has been the giant Surf

Pool where you can 'hang Ten' on 6 foot waves that come billowing from Mount Mayday, periodically erupting in huge tidal waves sure to sweep away unsuspecting swimmers. As with Disney's Blizzard Beach water park, you'll want to get there early to get a locker and to find a place in the shade near the spot in the park where you think you'll spend most of your time. Try to gauge where the sun is, and where it will be in a few hours and plan accordingly. You don't want to find a nice shady spot only to realize you'll soon be baking in the hot Florida sun!

Typhoon Lagoon features a variety of body slides and tube slides

In addition to the Surf Pool, Typhoon Lagoon features a number of attractions that are sure to keep you cool throughout the day. You can check out Keelhaul Falls and Mayday Falls on these single-rider tube slides, or take the plunge down Gangplank Falls in a giant four-person tube. The Humunga Kowabunga body slide (no tubes allowed) is a straight five-story plunge, and you can also check out the Storm Slides, a trio of body slides grouped together that each offer a unique plunge into the cool waters of Typhoon Lagoon. There are also a couple of fun attractions for kids too. Ketchakiddee Creek is a play area featuring slides and raft rides for the little ones, and the Bay Slides will treat tots to their own set of mini-thrills.

If you get hungry during your time in the park, there are a number of areas where you can grab a bite. Check out Leaning Palms, Lowtide Lou's or Typhoon Tilly's for sandwiches, burgers, and other snacks, or drop in to Crush Hot Dog or Surf Doggies for a turkey leg or hot dog. A couple of these locations also have a drink refill station you can leverage if you've purchased a refillable mug. If you're looking for adult beverages, stop by Let's Go Slurpin' to grab a cold one.

You can buy a day pass to Typhoon Lagoon for about $56 (including tax), or you can get tickets as part of the Water Park Fun & More add-on to your base ticket.

Top Attractions at Typhoon Lagoon

Surf Pool

This is the centerpiece of Typhoon Lagoon- a huge pool forming a quarter-circle that washes up to beach areas that surround it. The deepest part of the pool is six feet deep, and there are shallower areas on the side so those with small children can enjoy the waves- after they've been reduced to 'kiddie' proportions.

Unlike the Melt-Away Bay wave pool at Blizzard Beach, you won't find any tubes floating in the Surf Pool at Typhoon Lagoon. The waves are just too big- there would be tubes flying everywhere! Every couple of minutes, a siren sounds signaling the Typhoon is about to hit!

If you're in the deepest part of the pool, it can be VERY intimidating to see the huge six foot wall of water churning toward you. Some try to body surf on the waves, some try to dive beneath them. Either way, you'll find yourself being pulled away in the current.

Catch a wave at Typhoon Lagoon

NOTE: If you're a parent with little ones who may not be the strongest swimmers, or who may be small enough to really get thrown about by the waves, be careful! The waters are very turbulent and have pulled more than a few swimmers under. On our last trip we saw a little girl who was flipped face first into the bottom of the pool and came up crying with a bloody nose and several scrapes. Keep the kids close- and hold on!

Shark Reef

Shark Reef is great fun for the whole family. Disney supplies the mask, the snorkel, the coral reef- and the fish for an interesting one of a kind experience. Be forewarned- the water is kept at a chilly 68 degrees! Quite a change from the Surf Pool and water slides!

You enter the water in an area that's about 2 feet deep, where you get a quick lesson in snorkeling. It's a little tricky for first timers to get used to breathing through the snorkel, and you're likely to get a few mouthfuls of saltwater before you get the hang of it. It took the kids a couple times across the reef before they were comfortable with it.

Shark Reef

You'll get to see lots of cool fish- including sharks and stingrays as you traverse the pool. Near the end on the right side is the best place to go as many fish seem to hang out there. When you get to the end you have the option of keeping your snorkel and mask and going around again and again! We went through the pool three or four times each. Mom, who has the biggest fear of sharks, went across the most!

After you're done you can go to an underground path built like a sunken ship where you can look through the port holes to see the fish from a different perspective, and see the other swimmers take their turns.

Crush 'n' Gusher

Crush 'n' Gusher is one of the newest slides at Typhoon Lagoon, and also one of the coolest! You can choose to ride solo in a single person tube or with one or two partners in tubes that seat two or three people, and take the plunge down one of three different slides: Banana Blaster, Coconut Crusher, or Pineapple Plunger. Each slide is over 400 feet long!

Part of the ride takes place in an enclosed tube which then gives way to open areas. The dark parts are a bit scary because you can't see which dip or curve is coming next. No matter which slide you choose, the ride culminates in a big splash in the pool at the bottom!

Blizzard Beach

A blizzard has struck central Florida! While you're visiting Disney's Blizzard Beach, YOU get to reap the benefits! The Blizzard Beach water park has been a mainstay at Walt Disney World since its opening in April, 1995. It hosts around 2 million guests annually making it the 2nd most visited water park in the world- behind only Disney's own Typhoon Lagoon. Mount Gushmore is the centerpiece of this ski resort/water park filled with water slides, a lazy river, and even a chair lift that takes you to the top of the mountain.

Toboggan Racers at Blizzard Beach

As with Disney's Typhoon Lagoon water park, you'll want to get there early to get a locker and to find a place in the shade near the spot in the park where you think you'll spend most of your time. Try to gauge where the sun is, and where it will be in a few hours and plan accordingly. You don't want to find a nice shady spot only to realize you'll soon be baking in the hot Florida sun! Both parks also offer premium covered picnic area rentals should you want to sit down to a nice lunch and be guaranteed a seat in the shade.

In keeping with its ski resort theme, the attractions at Blizzard Beach are laid out in a series of color coded 'slopes'. Head to the Green Slope to ride the chairlift to the top of Mt. Gushmore. From there you can access the granddaddy of them all, Summit Plummet. You can also ride Slush Gusher and Teamboat Springs, a fun family raft ride, to the bottom from the summit. The Purple Slope hosts the Toboggan Racers and Snow Stormers slides, as well as the Downhill Double Dipper, a set of side-by-side racing slides. Finally, there's the Red Slope which features Runoff Rapids, a series of 600-foot tube slides full of twists and turns with a big splash at the bottom.

View of Blizzard Beach from the top of Summit Plummet

After you've 'hit the slopes', take some time to relax and cool down in Cross Country Creek, Blizzard Beach's lazy river that twists and turns throughout the park. Or grab a tube for a bit more excitement in Melt-Away Bay, Blizzard

Beach's one-acre wave pool nestled up against the base of Mt. Gushmore. Melt-Away Bay provides an experience that differs from Typhoon Lagoon's Surf Pool. It features a series of smaller, rolling waves rather than the giant Tsunami that sweeps you away in the Surf Pool. As with the Surf Pool, there are also areas at the sides of Melt-Away Bay where smaller children can enjoy the waves without being hit by their full force.

Speaking of the kiddies, there are a couple of areas at Blizzard Beach specifically designed for pre-teens and younger children too. The older kids will enjoy the Ski Patrol Training Camp featuring a variety of smaller slides and a really fun T-bar drop with a big splash at the end. Younger kids (48 inches tall or less) will enjoy Tike's Peak, a children's play area with a few smaller slides, a snow castle fountain play area, and a few pop (water) jets.

Ski Patrol Training Camp

Should all this splashing around make you hungry, there are a variety of options for food and snacks in the park. Avalunch, the Warming Hut, and Lottawatta Lodge offer a variety of light entrees, snacks and desserts, and each also features a drink refill station for those who have purchased souvenir refillable mugs. You can stop by Sled Dog Expeditions to grab an ice cream and soft drink too. If you seek an adult beverage, slalom on over to the Polar Pub or Frostbite Freddy's to wet your whistle.

You can buy a day pass to Blizzard Beach for about $56 (including tax), the same price as a day pass to Typhoon Lagoon, or you can get tickets as part of the Water Park Fun & More add-on to your Magic Your Way base ticket.

Top Attractions at Blizzard Beach

Summit Plummet

This is one water slide that's not for everyone- it's VERY intimidating! It's one big long straight drop at about a 60 degree angle, and you'll travel nearly 60 miles per hour on the way down. It's an atomic wedgie waiting to happen!

You start by waiting in a long, long line. When you get to the top of the hill you think you're almost there...but you're not. You still need to climb several flights of stairs at the platform. It's a very scenic view from the top as you tower over everything!

Summit Plummet

When you sit down at the top of the slide, the scariest part is that you can't see the slide no matter how far forward you lean. It's too steep. As you inch your way forward on the slide, you keep hoping you'll actually be able to see where you're going. Unfortunately, that never happens and suddenly... whoooooshh- down you go! It's quite an adrenalin rush on the way down but if you have the nerve to do it- you'll love it!

If you wear a swimsuit like this, you may get to the bottom before your suit does!

Note about bikinis: Unless you want to risk putting on a very un-family friendly show at the bottom of the slide, do NOT ride Summit Plummet in a skimpy string bikini. Chances are you'll lose one (or both!) of the pieces on your way down the slide. The force of the water at 60 mph is too much for the suit to handle. This happened on our last trip to the teenage girl in line in front of us- much to her (and her dad's) embarrassment. Luckily mom was waiting at the bottom of the slide with a towel ready so 'the show' was brief.

The lifeguard at the top said this happens about 30 times a day. Your best bet is to wear a one-piece bathing suit instead. You've been warned!

The whole family can take the plunge at Teamboat Springs

Teamboat Springs

According to Wikipedia, Teamboat Springs is the world's longest "family white-water raft ride" at 1,400 feet long. Not sure if anyone can confirm this (is that a record that's really tracked?) but I can tell you that Teamboat Springs is great fun for the entire family! After you climb the stairs (or take the chairlift) to the Green Slope at the top of Mt. Gushmore, you'll find Teamboat Springs just across the path from Summit Plummet and Slush Gusher. You and up to five others will climb aboard a large round rubber raft. You'll sit around the perimeter of the raft with your feet in the middle. You have only a few seconds to get situated and grab the handles before you are whooshed down the first hill before making a big splash in the white-water below.

Take the plunge into Teamboat Springs

Prepare yourself for a long run featuring plenty of twists and turns and high-banked curves as you head toward the bottom of the run. Since the raft is round, it has no front or back so you'll be facing forward sometimes and be completely blind to what comes next at other times as you slalom down the mountain backwards. It's a little unnerving when you're at the highest point of the raft on a high-banked turn looking straight down at your family and friends on the other side of the raft. There are lots of splashes and laughs on the way down with only a few slightly scary moments. All in all Teamboat Springs is a blast! You'll want to ride it again and again.

Meltaway Bay

Although there a lots of other great water slides at Disney's Blizzard Beach water park, you'll probably spend a lot of time at the Melt-Away Bay wave pool. This one acre wave pool nestled up to the foot of Mount Gushmore is quite a bit different than the Surf Pool at Disney's Typhoon

Lagoon water park. It's not as large as the Surf Pool at Typhoon Lagoon, and the waves are not as huge. These gently rolling waves will have you bobbing and drifting about, rather than simply blasting you over with the full force Tsunami-style waves of the pool at Typhoon Lagoon. It's also not as intimidating for youngsters- and cautious moms & dads.

There are plenty of tubes floating in the pool so you can ride the waves, but during busy times you may have to hunt for a recently abandoned one. The waves are a pretty good size (the closer you are to Mount Gushmore, the bigger the waves will be) and they're fun to ride on in one of the many tubes available. There are areas off to both sides of the pool where little ones will be shielded from the full force of the waves, and there are even a few waterfalls on the right side of the pool where you can relax and let the water pummel you. Another plus is that there are several shady areas near the pool where you can relax and cool off a bit.

Although the experience of the Melt-Away Bay wave pool is much different from that of the Surf Pool at Typhoon Lagoon, I find it to be a more enjoyable experience- especially if you just want to float around and relax.

Tikes Peak play area for smaller kids

7) Ready, Set, Go!

Your magical journey awaits

Congratulations! You now know everything you need to know to prepare for the ultimate adventure on your magical journey to Walt Disney World. You've learned all about how to plan your trip, how long to stay, and where to stay. I've given you the lowdown on each of the parks, and some of their "can't miss" attractions, and provided details about the many options for accommodations at Walt Disney World whether you're planning to stay at a Disney resort, or at one of the many hotels, condos, and resorts in the area. By now, you probably have an idea of how long you'd like to stay, and which ticket option is best for you and your family.

I truly hope you've enjoyed reading this second edition of Discover the Magic as much as I've enjoyed writing it. With double the content of the first edition, I hope you feel your time (and money) was well spent. I felt as if I were reliving each and every trip as the pages unfolded. I never had the chance to visit Disney as a kid, and now that I have a family of my own I don't think I'll ever get tired of going. Each trip is a little different than the last, and every trip brings new surprises, new adventures, and new memories that will last a lifetime.

If you purchased this book unsure as to whether a Disney vacation was for you, I hope I've helped you decide. If you were going to Disney anyway, I hope I've provided some valuable information to help you make the most of your vacation. While this book certainly couldn't cover every single detail of the parks, rides, and attractions, I'm sure you wouldn't want it to do so. A book that large would take forever to read, and you'll want to explore the parks and discover some of the magic yourself!

If you've enjoyed this book, I hope you'll share it with family & friends. I would love it if you would **please** visit the Amazon book page and post a review. It just takes a minute. If you scroll down the page and click the **Write a Customer Review** button it will help me share these experiences with others. I hope you will also "Like" my Disney Facebook page (https://www.facebook.com/DisneyVacations4Families)

and follow me on Twitter (@Disney4Families). If you'd like to see some great park videos including ride POVs, please subscribe to my YouTube channel (DisneyVacations4Fams) too. With so many changes constantly occurring at Disney, it's guaranteed that something will be different a few months down the road. I'll post many park updates on Facebook and Twitter, so that's the best way to keep in touch. This is also where I'll announce new books, updates, book sales and other promotions.

If you did not enjoy this book, please direct message me on Facebook and tell me how I've let you down. If there are details you were looking for that weren't there, or other things you feel I should add, please let me know. I would be happy to provide that information to you directly, or to include it in a future edition.

Thanks again for reading. Enjoy your trip, and have a magical day!

CPSIA information can be obtained at www.ICGtesting.com
Printed in the USA
LVOW04s1919020715

444768LV00033B/959/P